Books by Edward Weeks

THIS TRADE OF WRITING

THE OPEN HEART

IN FRIENDLY CANDOR

BREAKING INTO PRINT

BOSTON, CRADLE OF LIBERTY

THE LOWELLS AND THEIR INSTITUTE

FRESH WATERS

Collections edited by Edward Weeks

GREAT SHORT NOVELS

THE POCKET ATLANTIC

JUBILEE: 100 YEARS OF THE ATLANTIC
(with Emily Flint)

FRESH WATERS

FRESH WATERS

by

EDWARD WEEKS

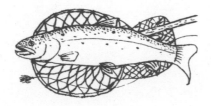

Drawings by WALTER DOWER

An Atlantic Monthly Press Book

LITTLE, BROWN AND COMPANY · BOSTON · TORONTO

ATLANTIC—LITTLE, BROWN BOOKS
ARE PUBLISHED BY
LITTLE, BROWN AND COMPANY
IN ASSOCIATION WITH
THE ATLANTIC MONTHLY PRESS

*Published simultaneously in Canada
by Little, Brown & Company (Canada) Limited*

PRINTED IN THE UNITFD STATES OF AMERICA

For James N. White and David McCord
whom it was such fun to follow

ACKNOWLEDGMENTS

IT would be quite impossible to name all those who have helped me during my thirty happy years of river life; those I have identified will not, I hope, regard me as intrusive or libelous. A feeling of inadequacy has at times restrained me from writing about other friends whose streams I fished only briefly. In preparing the book which was a labor of love, I have been indebted to Walter Dower, whose drawings catch the spirit of what I was trying to say; to Roderick Haig-Brown and to Dr. Lauren R. Donaldson of the University of Washington, who deepened my understanding of the rearing and protection of fish; to Virginia Albee, my secretary, whose interest in nature and conservation was an unfailing stimulant; to Peter Davison and Phoebe Lou Adams for their vigilant editing; and to my wife and son, whose impressions added spice to mine in so many of these adventures.

CONTENTS

FRESH WATERS

1. *THE RELUCTANT BEGINNER*

YOU must understand that up to my fortieth birthday I looked on fishing as the most economical way of providing the table with that menu of clams — raw, steamed, or fried — lobster, and scrod which is native to Boston. That there was any grace or rapture in the business of catching fish I failed to perceive either in my study of Winslow Homer's paintings or on my repeated visits to a restaurant as savory as the Old Union Oyster House. Fish were for eating, and so they remained until the spring of 1938 when like St. Paul on the road to Ephesus I had an encounter and, rather against my better judgment, began to see things differently. I entered timidly into my new life but like all converts I became eager to tell others of what it feels like to be among the redeemed.

I suppose that the Christians from the Catacombs were not the easiest people in Rome to listen to. It must have been so difficult to get them to talk about anything else. I well remember, in the days before I was saved, with what incredulity bordering on disdain I listened to the credo of those known to be masters of the fly rod: that an artist as sensitive as Leslie P. Thompson, an editor as sophisticated as Ferris Greenslet, a bookseller as shrewd as Richard B. Fuller, proprietor of the Old Corner Bookstore, could attach such importance to their words about dry flies, Green Highlanders, 4-ounce rods, and Hardy leaders was in defiance of commonsense. I liked these elders and enjoyed playing backgammon and golf with them, and always the cocktail hour, but even as we were relaxing over the 19th hole, back would come that far look in their eyes and this cult-talk which sounded to me as mysterious as sex but not nearly so much fun. I did not realize until much later that what they were speaking was the private language of their double life, the symbol of those hours when, remote from their professional calling and domesticity, they were worshipping in the cathedral quiet of a clean-run trout stream.

Evidently my disdain was not lost on them for in June I had the encounter I have referred to and it was at their insistence. I was told to bring along fifty dollars, and in their company at an outfitters on Washington Street, Boston, I was advised in the purchase of a 9-foot bamboo fly rod, all-purpose and inexpensive, a reel, line and a dozen small flies, gaily feathered. Included was an invitation to spend the following weekend with them in Dick Fuller's cabin in the woods not far from Scituate on the North River, where it was hoped we would do some business with the striped bass, schools of which were coming upstream on the high tide. Why not? I thought, at least there'll be plenty of liquor.

Dick's cabin was built on the foundation of an old mill and of its contents I recall the four bunks, the open fire, icebox, and Let Thompson's guitar. Before the cocktails Ferris led me out to the causeway, mounted my rod, supplied a tapered gut leader of 9 feet for my little streamer fly of red and white and on the quiet millpond gave me my first lesson in casting and retrieving. Being a tennis player I tried to serve with the rod, bearing down with the fly too hard and too soon. "It's all done with the forearm," said Ferris. "Pick the fly up with your wrist, slow back, count three, and as you come forward, give it the wrist again. Look!" and he demonstrated, his fly falling as lightly as if it were a berry dropping from an overhanging bough. I felt clumsy after that and said so. "Don't worry," said the Duke, who thought in literary terms, "you'll be using it like a pencil before you're much older."

After the steak which our host broiled on the open fire, and the coffee, Let began strumming up his favorite tunes while the Duke and I wiped. Then there was talk about tomorrow in which I could detect the anticipation. "Wonder where we'll find 'em," said Dick, as he blew out the lamp, "in the estuary, or upstream?"

To those who don't know them fishermen pass as patient folk. Truth is they are as irascible as most but have learned composure. To me my tutors seemed imperturbable on that bright June morning which grew ever hotter under the soft southwesterly. We rode the outgoing tide downriver, trolling seaworms, and sand eels on leaded hooks that would swing them close to the bottom; we passed the ruined shipways that had once launched famous clippers, circled the river mouth, and then coasted offshore, and except for one small pollock, quickly returned, all we caught was sunburn. The air of expectancy never abated. "They got to be somewhere," said Dick.

High noon brought a respite. We anchored on a sand spit at a decent distance from the summer cottages, stripped, and went for a swim. The glare of the sun, the diamond points dancing on the water made one squint. Martinis, cold from the thermos, added just the right moisture to the thin ham and Swiss cheese sandwiches and brought on some reminiscence. "Reminds me of the time I was trolling for stripers in the Ipswich River," Ferris remarked with one of his characteristic grunts. We waited. "Got a mixed bag. Early in the morning picked up a pollock, little smaller than that one of Let's; later, on the eel flats opposite Castle Hill, I hooked an old sneaker, and in the afternoon upriver where they go canoeing I tied into a condum. Sneaker put up the best fight." We hooted.

Refreshed and relaxed we resumed our vigil in the open cockpit. Back and forth we cruised, back and forth. There were no terns dipping and slapping at the water to show where fish were feeding, just a single gull now and then, high and morose. Dick swept the horizon with his binoculars but to no avail. I could feel the back of my neck getting

redder and stiffer by the hour. It was impossible to be bored
in that company, but a novice could be excused for feeling
impatient and though I tried not to show it, I was. Not so
my companions: they changed places, put on fresh bait,
smoked and chaffed, unshaken in their belief that this
tedium of no-fish could be broken at any moment.

The breeze had dropped as we headed back upriver in
the face of the lowering sun. I thought we were calling it a
day, but no, we churned past our landing and reduced
speed as we followed the winding, narrowing stream. The
tide was high, the unruffled water at the very lip of the
marsh whose vivid green was in natural harmony with the
darkening water and azure sky, their air so still that a child's
voice or the challenge of a dog identified the home con-
cealed in the trees. We made an S curve and entered a long
stretch with a couple of big boulders showing midway and a
broad pool deep in the reeds at the end of the corridor. But
we never reached it. For as our lines drew level with the
rocks Ferris's rod bowed and his reel chattered, and at the
same instant I felt a powerful swipe underwater. "Ted's
got one, too," cried Dick. "Upp — you've lost him. Reel
in."

In that still green setting as the tide turned we had found
our stripers, strong and gleaming fresh, three to five pounds,
with that clearly discerned stripe that gives them their nickname. There must have been thousands feeding in that half-
mile stretch; on each run as we neared the rocks we had a
strike — though not always the fish — and after we had

boated five, Let asked to be put ashore on the marsh so that he could cast for them with a fly. None came to his Gray Ghost, but in that setting to watch the grace and deliberation of that sturdy figure was a joy.

Our endurance through the long day from the bright hope of morning to the glare of noon had brought us to this evening of reward. Love is pictures and my mind's eye was to hold thereafter my initial exposure to that swirling power underwater which called out something latent in me, the restful fusion of marsh and river at full tide, and the beauty with which Let cast and retrieved, the sudden arc as the line lifted and flew behind him, the delicacy with which he placed his fly. A single vision is enough for most converts.

After my second lesson on the millpond that evening I followed the example of the others and washed the brine off the varnished bamboo, soaked my line in fresh water and rubbed a coating of oil on my reel. "Salt water is no good for fresh-water gear," said Dick. "Always wash it off. You're going to have fun with that rod."

2. *FISHING IN THE BACKYARD*

THE possession of a bamboo rod does not make an angler, nor do three lessons in casting on a millpond. I had seen just enough of the rod in competent hands to realize how many hundreds, no thousands of hours of experience I was short. Shyness for a time restrained me from inviting myself on other expeditions. No beginner will willingly show off before a pro and it would be years before I ceased to be self-conscious on a stream. But fishing with one's family is not invidious, especially if Pa talks as if he really knew.

That summer we explored the little brooks and the ponds, great and small, within a ten-mile radius of our cottage in Essex County, north of Boston. We took turns with the rod, used what the elite refer to as "garden tackle," meaning worms (dug from the compost heap), and were as happy to net a white perch or large-mouth bass as we were the rarer brook trout. I had taken to heart the essay "On Fishing with a Worm," by Bliss Perry, my predecessor once removed on the *Atlantic*, and it was a surprise to find how many streams in our neighborhood held fish the natives had forgotten about.

We began with the overgrown brook that burrowed its way through the backyards of Beverly Farms. Someone told me that in the dim past salters used to come up it each spring. Salters? Yes, sea trout that return to fresh water in the spring. Well, it seemed silly to dabble publicly in shallows everyone else took for granted, so I tracked upstream a mile and a half to a spot of concealment where the brook penetrated a stand of oaks at the rear of an enormous greenhouse, strongly fenced and long famous for its orchids. The owner, who was one of my golfing partners, said he had never seen a trout taken there but was quite agreeable to have me try, and passed the word to his overseer. Buried Aztec-deep in dock, iris, alder, and bull brier was a remarkable layout: a pool fifteen yards across, with stone steps leading down to it, an ancient Chinese lantern of stone, and a high-curved Oriental bridge arching over the deep and narrow connecting link that led into a second pool, muddy, bosky, with a tiny temple disguising the outlet. At the bottleneck between the pools an alder with many branches had broken through the masonry; if there were trout anywhere they'd be under that witchy tree. The problem was how to reach them. I recrossed the Chinese bridge, plunged into the breast-high growth, and pressing through it came upon a flat stone bench on the parapet directly opposite the alder. Standing on the bench I found I could get a good pendulum swing for my line with its well-hooked worm, weighted with a single buckshot. On my first cast I dunked it into the shadowed water, the line flickered this way and that as it sank, I felt a sharp tug and instantly I reared back and derricked a fat trout over my shoulder and into the jungle behind me. Part of the fun of the thing was finding the fish in the thicket, for it disappeared out of sight as swiftly as if it had gone back to water. For my first prize I dropped the rod and dove into the undergrowth until I found the flapping tail. None of this was in accordance with what Ferris had taught me, but it had the thrill of discovery.

The trout were golden-bellied, beautifully spotted, and as hungry as if they had been unmolested for years. Three an evening — I stopped here repeatedly on the way home from the office — was our maximum catch, and for each fish landed there were several we missed, and such a welter of mosquito bites as made the scratching last. Unaccountably there would be still evenings when no fish moved. My log book shows a total of twenty-three for that first spring and we did not crow about our trouvé, fearing the law of diminishing returns. The trout varied in size and we occasionally got glimpses of a large one which came to be known as "Pa's Fish" because it eluded my best efforts, and which was finally captured when I was in England by the combined cunning of my wife and young Ted. The letter that brought me the news added the consoling note that

Fritzy fell off the stone bench into the deep hole while trying to land him.

The fact that Pa's fish was thought to be the largest and that my claims on him were coveted is an index of the competitive spirit that develops so quickly even in family fishing. I believe I have it subdued but I am never sure.

In those days the trout season in Massachusetts came to a close at the end of July (a law which had it prevailed would have preserved countless native trout throughout the Northeast) and when "Orchidvale" became off limits we took our rod in search of fresh water bass or perch. Half a mile from our cottage our neighbor Harry McKean had a small roadside pond, the digestive playground of a haughty flock of Canada geese. "D'you think there are any fish in it?" I telephoned. Harry hadn't the foggiest idea but said I was free to try provided I didn't bring the populace down on him. My first trial was at dusk when there were few cars on the road and the most I accomplished was a tentative armistice with the geese. The largest gander tried to drive me off, wings outstretched, neck low and hissing, but as I retreated only a little and did not strike back with my long weapon, he came to tolerate me as a temporary nuisance.

On the water I saw long arrows, not caused by the wind, make a pass at my streamer fly or flee from it as it hit the water, and on a subsequent visit with the sun still on the water and the geese elsewhere I teased a bass into attacking my Gray Ghost. It was a perfect place to cast and my aim and length were improving though the splash no less. But, alas, I was observed. On a Sunday an Italian family appeared, spinning rods, glass bobbers, plenty of bait and their lunch; taking their stand close to the road, in case of sudden exit, they proceeded to dredge up five bass going two pounds or better — and that was the end of Harry's patience and my sanctuary. The geese took back their domain.

Spread through the pine woods that cover the moraine reaching almost to Gloucester are a number of great ponds, and to two of these, the Ice House Pond and our favorite, the better-hidden Round Pond, we went for Sunday picnics with a canoe we had borrowed from the MacNichols. (We seem to have been inveterate borrowers at this stage.) It would take two trips to ferry our lunch, the gear and Mickey, the black spaniel, over to the grassy point where we would boil our lobsters and green corn and then stretch out waiting for the shadows to lengthen. The beech and pine on the ridge put the little coves on the western shore in shade by three, and it was there from the canoe that we began casting toward the shore, avoiding the reeds where the pickerel lay for the rock-covered stretches where we hoped to catch a bass. What we hooked were perch, small bass, and crappies the size of a butterplate. Rarely, getting on toward six o'clock we might hit the lair of a larger fish who would roil the water and so excite us that invariably we pulled the fly away from him. We would have done better with a plug, much better with nightcrawlers, the juiciest of worms, but we were dedicated to learning how to handle our fly rod, as it passed from Ted or Fritzy taking turns in the bow to me in the stern. My daughter Sara, who had been at boarding school, never really caught the bug as we did. But she came along on the picnics, sketched or swam while we were fishing, and being an excellent cook earned her keep over the campfire.

As I paddled along the shore we came to know the underwater architecture of Round Pond. There was one gray rockface on the eastern shore where the white perch had their apartments; they preferred worms to a streamer, and, though shy, were occasionally to be taken here. There were two rocky points reaching deep into the pond and perhaps four hundred yards apart: in this dark water and at certain times under the waterlilies closer to shore dwelt the bass. We saw them surface-feeding, and on rare evenings we angered the big ones; while in the shallows at the outlet the whole cove was overpopulated with stunted yellow perch and crappies. For us, of course, the bass were the aristocrats, so were they for one dark, burly man from Lynn who occasionally showed up in a small skiff and who would sit for hours off one of the rocky points with two rods out, bottom fishing with shiners for bait. He captured the only large fish we were ever to see out of water, a small-mouthed bass of three pounds and we paddled over and touched it and were momentarily envious.

We were learning also, though we had few words for it at the time, the spectrum of color that makes revisiting an intimate pond so refreshing. Here were the wild azalea in the spring and the cardinal flower in the summer, the wild honeysuckle and the bees, the waterlilies white and pink, and latest of all the swamp maples as they turned scarlet in September. Loveliest were the evening shadows as the light

fell and the fish rose, and you were taking your last casts —
damn the bugs! — with a sliver of moon riding up in the
sky.

Women generally know their way around in the dark but
there was one thing I never could teach Fritzy: when the
time came to load that slippery canoe on the top of the car
I naturally took the upper end since I have the long arms,
but no amount of my advice could keep the water and fish-
scales out of her hair.

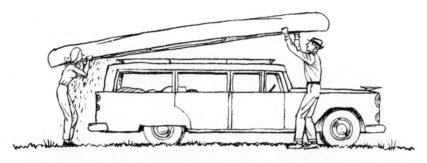

One rod is not enough for a threesome and my impulse
to take it out of others' hands when a fish showed and a
crisis impended did not add to our harmony. The solution
was to find another, which we did almost on the anniversary
of my initiation. When I talked it over with my good friend
James N. White, he paused and then said, "Weeksie, how
would you like to buy my old Thomas? I've grown very
fond of the Payne which the kids gave me last Christmas
and I don't think I've used my old rod once this spring.
Must have fished with it for twenty years, but it's in good
shape. We'll ask Stoddard's to set the price, and I'll throw
in the Pfluger reel and my old silk line." It was a deal.

I doubt if there was any common possession except
Mickey about which the three of us came to feel so affec-
tionate as this, our first Thomas rod. It stood 8 feet and

weighed close to 5 ounces but the balance was so true that you would hardly have guessed it was as heavy as that. Best of all it had a stiff backbone and gave one good distance even in the face of gusty spring winds. We wiped it after each outing, varnished it anew at the beginning of each season, and though I never actually took it to bed with me after a happy day, there were evenings when I felt like it.

We only know how deeply we care for a child after it has been in grave peril, a realization that came home to us in mid-May. The three of us had gone for an evening picnic on the Ipswich River, borrowing one of the Steward's canoes and having our sandwiches and coffee aboard ship. Now the sun had gone down and Ted and I were paddling home in the semi-dark, making hard work of it against the strong current which kept shoving us in a diagonal course between the maples and the alders that lined the bank. "Come on, pick it up, Ted!" I grunted at him as I shifted my paddle and dug in on his side. He looked back to remonstrate; then his face changed and he cried out in warning. I had stowed the Thomas behind me in the stern, the fly in its appointed ring and the top half above the gunwale, but as we brushed close to one of the maples — Maple No. 9 — a strong tendril had inserted itself between the line and the rod and I looked around just in time to see the rod drawn out of the canoe and deposited without a trace in the dark water. It was too late that night to do anything more than mark the spot and we went home in mute despair. At eight the next morning — it had come on to rain — Ted and I, with Fritzy to cheer us, paddled back to the same spot in bathing suits that were plenty chill. From a friend who was a skin diver we had borrowed a pair of rubber feet to help us search the bottom. Ted believed the rod must have been swept downstream under the force of the current, so he began diving below the Ninth Maple, but without avail. Then we paddled a bit upstream from the marked spot and it was my turn. Six times in succession I dove and kicked my way down, actually rubbing my long beak on the sandy bottom and desperately grasping at waterlogged sticks, pebbles, or nothing, and then in one last convulsive reach I touched the small, smooth tip of the rod and light as a feather it came up in my hand as I surfaced. Of all those square inches of sandy bottom how did I ever touch that one? The gods were on our side.

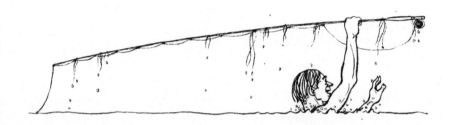

3. *FIRST TIME NORTH*

FISHING friends are long friends because the doing of it is an intense perceptive preoccupation and one that is charged with unexpected humor. Every family has a treasury of stories, little adventures, that gather color the more they are retold, and of families that fish together this is particularly true.

Ever since their birth my daughter Sara and young Ted had had unofficial godparents in my contemporaries Jim White — "Uncle Fudge" as Sara christened him — and David McCord, the poet, who soon became "Uncle Dave." Dave had the mate of the Thomas rod I had just bought from Jim as these two had begun fishing together when they were classmates at Harvard. Now twenty years later I was being admitted to their fraternity, and it fell to "Uncle Dave" to take us to their old stamping ground, Kennebago.

This was our first visit to northern trout water and each impression beginning with the parking of our cars at the head of the lake and the long outboard trip to Grant's Camps was etched on fresh plates. We were in the Valley of the Blue Mountains with almost three hundred miles of wilderness between our lake and Quebec and Dave gave us the lay of the land as we hummed along — off to our right was the mountain trail on which the uncorrupted Benedict Arnold had led his tough little expeditionary force for the assault on Quebec, the exploit Kenneth Roberts had written about in his novel *A Rabble in Arms*. Dave indicated the fishing grounds: explained how the tributary, Little Kennebago, which lay to the north of us, and the Boneyard, the narrow, deep connecting link, provided even better fishing than the big lake when the wind was right, and how the outlet at our end formed Kennebago Stream in which beside trout there were landlocked salmon, strong as mischief, going up to six pounds and usually to be taken on a dry fly. (We had never cast a dry fly.) The sun was setting behind the western range with the fire ranger's lookout in silhouette as we curved up to the dock and there to greet us and help with our gear was Jim O'Brien, the guide whom Dave with admirable forethought had asked for in advance.

Jim O'Brien was a genial, thick-set Hibernian who

knew every mood of these waters and in the seven days to come he was our pace-setter and Paul Bunyan. He paddled young Ted whom he had taken under his wing while Dave and I paddled Fritzy, but as the canoes were never far apart we all shared in his advice. Each morning Ted would be in a lather to land the first fish, casting eight times to the minute, and to calm him down Jim would remark, "Ted, there's an old saying: 'You'll never catch a trout with your hook in the air.' " As the sun warmed the surface and the trout went deep, Jim would lead us to a shoal in mid-lake where he showed us how to dredge: stripping out the line and letting it sink until the fly was close to the bottom, then retrieving it in short jerks. When Ted's line got fouled in the process, Jim took over the rod, straightened out the snarl, made a far cast, waited, and then dredged into a good fish, saying, as he handed back the bowed rod, "Look what you had on your line, son — why didn't you pull him up!" And if dredging failed at bright noon, we crossed the lake to a spring hole called the Nursery where Dave would show us how to roll the little ones over with his dry fly until he had just the right size for our trout chowder.

Jim cooked the delectable chowder at a shady campsite — onions, thin-sliced potatoes, and fifteen small trout, skinned, boned, and delectable as they were brewed in the milk. Trout chowder, toast, crisp bacon, blueberries, spice cake, and coffee — and then a stretch-out under the balsam. A Canada jay would join us within five minutes and sometimes a doe, on familiar terms with Jim, would come through the blueberry patch and wait for leavings.

We came off the water at sunset for cocktails but not Ted, skinny and persistent, who would remain at the end of the float, casting and lashing away. Guests had been known to catch lunkers off the dock and his turn might come; once he came running to us with a 10-incher: "Pa, he'd have put up a hell of a fight if I hadn't caught him on the backcast!"

It was the dry fly we all wanted to master and it was Dave who set the example. Our log cabin faced north and the view of the green heights and the deep shadows with the loon calling across the water was mighty gratifying whether at dawn or in the half-hour before supper. Between us and the water was a short stretch of turf with a low gray rock in the center on which one evening a grandfather frog had come to rest. "Watch this," said Dave. He took his rod from the pegs, tied on a dry fly with a barbless hook and cast the white moth just to the right of the throne. Old Frog's eyes became more protuberant as the white fluff came into his vision and finally he heaved himself around to have a better look. Whereupon Dave retrieved and placed the fly to the left of the rock. Old Frog was immovable but he heard the faint rustle and with great deliberation, like a member of the Union Club heaving himself out of a deep chair, he hoisted himself to the left. There the moth was and he glowered at it and there it wasn't for Dave had again

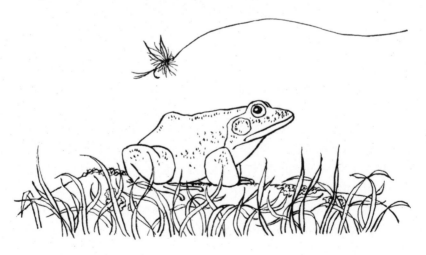

tossed it to his blind side. The next turnabout took time, began ponderously, but never stopped, for Old Frog's dander was up and this time he leapt right on the irritant, seized it in his mouth, spat it out and then with dignity resumed his throne. Our laughter did nothing to placate him.

The days of practice at the Nursery and in the Boneyard gave us the beginning of confidence for the pools in the Kennebago Stream where our hopes for raising a good salmon — any salmon — were so often thwarted by the perverse wind. Instead of a long straight line with my dry fly, dropping close to the opposite bank, I'd end up with a tangle of lace in the center of the pool. It took a quiet remark of Jim's to ease my exasperation one hot afternoon. "River's full of fish," he said, "and you'll get one if you rest the pool. Might even get that six-pounder that's got so many hooks in him they wanted him for the scrap drive." (This was wartime and metal, like gasoline, was short.)

Everything about the northern birds was new to us: the hooting mockery of the loons, the hungry curiosity of the Canada jays, the scratchy whisper of the nighthawks swooping low over the canoe as dark fell. Black duck and golden-eyes rose as our boat probed the lagoon of the Boneyard where the great gray skeletons of the trees traced the forest that was, before the lumbermen cut and flooded the valley. Sheer white against the spruce-lined banks was a pair of egrets — the first, the natives told us, ever to venture this far north. Now I began listing in our log a tally of the birds we'd seen each day. Kennebago showed us our first eagle.

As we gained more confidence in wading, we came to favor the pools in Kennebago Stream, especially for evening picnics when in the silver half-light the fish were moving and feeding, and when our awkward casting of the dry fly would be swiftly straightened out by the stream itself. Many clumsy anglers do their best at dusk.

The walk home along the dusky road was made memorable by the story-telling of Dave and Jim O'Brien. One evening as we paused to look at Canoe Pool, Dave pointed to a deep shadowy recess under a half-fallen tree. "Jimmy White and I came by here one evening at about this same time and there under that tree was the biggest ring you ever saw, a big fish feeding at regular intervals. We both had our limit and were aware of it, but Jimmy said, 'Go on, Dave, put on a small white moth and see if he'll take it.' He came all right and my he was a good fish, bigger than any we'd seen; he horsed around the pool and by the time Jimmy netted him he was exhausted. I got the fly out quickly, but when we put him back he started to turn belly up. So while Jimmy propped him under water, moving him back and forth to regain his oxygen, I built a little cradle of sticks strong enough to hold him upright. We put the trout in it and now we could see he was breathing. Then a nighthawk went over us whistling as he searched for insects; we looked up and when we looked down again the big trout had gone."

Jim O'Brien's gravity was forever fooling us: he spoke so seriously that we were never prepared. "Want to hear me call a moose?" he asked one twilight as we were trudging toward home. We stopped. He scanned the horizon, fixed his eyes on a distant point, cupped his lips, took a prodigious breath, and said, "Here, moosey, moosey, moosey." Coming from a six-foot two-hundred-and-twenty-pounder, it was wonderfully silly.

Another time he had been telling us about the great forest fires of a year ago. "They were bad," he said, "real bad." A pause. "Did you hear about the herd of deer up here got caught with smoke and cinders in their eyes? Blinded. But there was one young buck who could see; he lined them up and led six of them across the river each holding on to the other's tail. Then a guide crept up, cut the buck's tail, led the does into camp, and had himself enough deer's meat to last all winter."

Our family unit with Jim and Dave was self-contained and it was only at breakfast or at supper not on the stream that we compared notes with the other guests. From the old timers I heard an occasional reference to "the Big Night," a night devoutly to be wished for at about this time of year, when the mayflies appeared and the lake was turned inside out by feeding fish. We prayed that it would strike during our visit and it did on the Friday before our departure. Luckily for us we had elected to stay in camp instead of picnicking on the river.

It began like the ending of any other clear sunny June day except that after supper while we were sitting on the cabin porch mayflies were silhouetted in the afterglow of the sunset, more and more of them until they seemed to darken the swarming air. Mayflies in motion are like graceful flying spiders; they tend to hover so that you can almost count the r.p.m.'s of their wings. The guides came running and the canoes burst out on the ring-covered water racing for the rocky shoal where they anchored. We were all using artificial mayflies and it mattered little whether they rode high or floated half-submerged for their like was everywhere.

If there was a single trout not feeding on the surface that evening it was only because he was resting his mouth after a sharp encounter earlier in the day. But nature was too prodigal. There was simply too much even for gluttons. You would cast over a good rise only to see another and larger just beyond, yet the moment you lifted your fly, false cast to dry it and put it over the larger fish, a swarm of natural mayflies dropped on the water. The wiseheads, with enormous restraint, concentrated fixedly on one fish, but tenderfeet like ourselves, never imagining that there could be such myriads of eager fish, were soon thrashing in a frenzy. (The only sizable one we caught in my boat was false-hooked; David, who was with Jim, did distinctly better.) I felt like one of those Alaskan bears in Walt Disney's famous film, standing erect, swatting distractedly at the Pacific salmon that were coursing between his legs and just out of reach. It was the most chastening experience we had at Kennebago. We still had a lot to learn.

4. *DAM CAMP*

O UR trip to the north country did not lessen our zest for the waters close to Boston, rather it imbued us with a dream we have pursued ever since: to visit a new stream in a new terrain whenever possible. Meanwhile we did what we could to lengthen the season. Jamaica Pond, on the border between Brookline and Boston, was a stone's throw from the home of Mayor James Michael Curley. Into the pond were dumped each year the live trout and salmon exhibited at the Sportsman's Show and before their submersion the Mayor always had himself photographed with one of the larger salmon which had, I suspect, been tethered for this purpose. Since Jamaica Pond has deep, cold springs the discards survived and were joined each March with a seeding of small put-and-take hatchery trout. The pond could be fished as soon as the ice went out but only with a special permit from the Governor, which with editorial politesse I secured. We scouted the pond from the Parkway and the morning after the last of the ice disappeared, in our heavies, wristlets, and gloves Ted and I left Beacon Hill at 4:45 A.M. determined to be the first. We were. The dark was fading when we roused the little old woman in charge of the boathouse; in her wrapper she provided us with the oars for boat No. 3 and some half-frozen night crawlers, and I had taken a few strokes toward the little island in the center of the pond when the second customer showed up in a taxi, with its lights on.

The fish must have been as cold as we were, for nothing stirred. When the sun rose we shifted to streamer flies but it was hard casting. "Pa," said Ted, "what's wrong with my rod? The line won't run out." I looked, and the guides — the eyelets through which the line is supposed to pass —

were frozen solid. At eleven o'clock we went home for a second breakfast, skunked.

We continued to explore Essex County, finding trout in the little brook that ran from Centerville through the abandoned golf links of the old Montserrat Club, finding nothing but eels in the brook at South Byfield but a surprising colony of large-mouth bass in a sheltered pond I shall call "X," since we still frequent it, thanks to the hospitality of Bob and Barbara Livermore. This is a pond for all seasons and with its swamp maples its glory is in the fall. The bass run up to 5 pounds and after the first cool nights in September a cork popping bug, painted yellow or red, will produce fierce assaults from the lily pads.

I must salute the year that my mentor, Jim White, became a member of the Miramichi Fish and Game Club. The Northwest Miramichi is an early-run salmon river, a fast, narrow stream cutting its way through the Fraser Forest and then slowing its pace as it winds through the water meadows of New Brunswick to Newcastle and the sea. The Club is a small one with the prime fishing in June and the first half of July; its members draw lots for their nine or ten day allocation and it was Jim's generosity to invite Dave and myself to share his first five days at Dam Camp. Inexpert as I was this meant that I'd be moving up a class into heavier water for heavier fish.

For my novitiate Jim advised me to buy a Montague

grilse rod (a grilse is a small salmon returning for the first time from the sea to his native stream at a weight of 3 or 4 pounds). "The Montague is strong enough to hold anything you're likely to get," Jim said with a smile in his voice, "and it's a good rod to learn with. Bring your boots, a pair of rubber-soled shoes, and plenty of heavy socks. We fish from rocky stands, not from boats, and you'll be using your feet hard." Words to conjure with.

The fun of being a tenderfoot is that everything — including the mistakes — is for the first time. Our rendezvous was Fredericton, New Brunswick, and I made the overnight trip from Boston aboard *The Gull,* a sleeper of character, now defunct, which always played host to anglers at this time of year and which excited their appetites by slowing down as it approached any good-looking body of water as if to see if the fish were rising. For breakfast *The Gull* would pause at McAdam, five miles north of the border; that vast granite station of the Canadian Pacific, with its upper floor of incongruous guest rooms, had a cheery dining room with the eggs deliciously fresh, the coffee strong and hot, and here one could spot the sports in their flannel shirts and gabardines and that glow of expectancy of fishermen who hope to be on the water before dark. Much comparing of notes as to what rivers we were headed for and then the conductor would shepherd us aboard and after clearing Customs it was only a moderate run to the junction where those bound for Fredericton changed cars. Crossing the platform we passed trucks stacked high with narrow wooden coffins where, packed in ice and moss, and slightly leaking, were the salmon taken by parties already upriver, and now being sent to friends in the States. How much anticipation can one hold?

Fredericton is everything that a salmon capital should

be. It also happens to be the capital of the Province of New Brunswick, a barracks town of the eighteenth century — the Mounties have a headquarters there today — and once the refuge of Loyalist regiments and their families fleeing from the American Revolution. The British Crown paid the expenses of the exodus — Queens, a hamlet close to Fredericton, marks the settlement of almost an entire regiment, from colonel to drummer boy, wives included, from Queens, Long Island — and the little museum in the barracks displays some of the small silver the émigrés brought with them, along with regimental badges, ivory-handled swagger-sticks, and pieces of their furniture. But it was a sad retreat: the settlers built their cabins too close to the river and were flooded in the freshet; those from Manhattan did not take to farming, and by the third year they were again on the move to Halifax or Britain.

Today with the broad St. John at its doorstep, with the finest of the vanishing elms in North America, whose overlacing boughs were dripping with glossy foliage when I first saw them; and with Neill's, that sportsmen's haven where you buy your license, and Hardy flies before crossing the river, today it is the exhilarating take-off point for anglers bound for the Northwest or Southwest Miramichi, the Renous, the Cairns, the Sevogle, and half a dozen other tributaries.

For the members and guests of the Club the heartland of Fredericton was the home of Dr. Alex Bell, facing the Cathedral Green. Here those about to enter the woods paused to get the word, embellished by the Doctor's martinis, and here those homeward-bound paused to bathe, don their city clothes and tell of their exploits before sitting down to one of Cannie Bell's famous chicken dinners. When the two parties coincided as they did on my first visit with the George Munfords coming out, it was a big do full of laughter, teasing and affection.

Alex mixed his martinis in a great shaker in the form of a silver dinner bell and when the glasses were first filled he raised his and gave his favorite toast: "I looks toward ye, and lifts me glass, and smiles and bows according." Looking at him over your glass you saw what you were never to forget: his gay blue eyes set in the fresh pink complexion, and the well-shaped bald dome with its blond fuzz gave him the appearance of a stout, jovial Kewpie. He was one of a vanishing tribe, a general practitioner, known the length of the St. John River valley and in the fishing villages and lumber camps to Newcastle and beyond; he drove like Jehu — sometimes with an admonishing Mountie on his tail — and probably he had to with such distances to cover. He was, as I was to discover, the best beloved man in the Province and, when his dander was up and the rasp came into his voice, a fighter respected throughout the Maritimes and in Ottawa. Everyone knew Alex Bell, and the Club was fortunate in having him as a member and liaison officer with the government and the guides.

I was getting my bearings that first evening in a room full of strangers; their talk, as sophisticated as any I had heard from my elders in Boston, of salmon, seen, hooked, or lost at "the Top of the Falls," in "the Basin," or at "Mountain Brook," pictured a river and a skill I did not know. "George killed his limit the first morning," someone said — "killed," not "landed," or "netted," just "killed." I must remember. I felt less alone when Jim and Dave drove in and were welcomed, and I was touched when just before our departure, Dr. Bell drew me aside and pressed into my hand a small envelope containing two green and orange flies. "Green Highlanders, No. 6," he said, "they're my favorite for the Nor'west; they'll raise fish when nothing else will. Tight lines!" Handshakes all around and we were on the road. I had purchased four flies at Neill's, now I had six; furthermore I had two Hardy leaders of thin blue gut, 9 feet long and costing $1.75 each. This was expensive business.

We made the run north in the dark to a motel on the outskirts of Newcastle, the road under the new moon a black straight ribbon between the close-pressing conifers; a few sparse settlements hugging the road and dimly lit but always it seemed we were crossing streams which Jim named as we took the bridges: the Nashwaak, the broad Southwest, the Renous, and the Northwest. As we drove he told us about tomorrow. "We'll make an early start," he said, "should check in with the gate-keeper of the Forest by eight if we want to wet a line before lunch. He'll telephone the guides at Stony Brook and they'll be on the trail to meet us. I want you both to fish Stony Brook Pool, so we'll spend the first night there and then fish our way up-river to Dam Camp."

He told us about the river: "The Nor'west has one of the earliest runs of any of the Canadian streams, the sea-trout come first, and they've been taken before the end of May. They go through to the redds — the spawning beds — in two days. Then comes the first run of the mature salmon — this is a nine-pound river; that's about what they average. Then a second run of salmon and grilse — you'll often see a hen salmon and a male grilse traveling together.

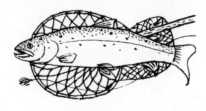

The grilse are the tough young bachelors and, boy, how they fight! After that the run becomes predominantly grilse until the river gets really low in early August when a long ledge below camp shuts off any further migration. If luck's with us the best fishing right now should be in the pools at Dam Camp." On that big "if" we went to sleep, all set for the six o'clock call.

It was warm and bright even by seven when we were on the road, a rough road in a cloud of dust with the loose stones whanging off our fenders. I noticed the pointed spruce, the incredibly long lines of laundry strung out to dry from an upper window of the home to a post in the yard — "Long winters, big families," remarked Dave laconically — I noticed the boy casting in the shadows underneath the bridge — how clean and good-looking were the children and girls at the roadside — and that the gate, where Jim dismounted to sign us in, was painted white with a red trim and that the rope to raise it passed through the wall of the gate house so that it could be lowered from within in stormy weather. I had no way to clock my anticipation but it was rising.

Then followed many miles of a road so potted and water-gullied it was a wonder we didn't break a spring. The surface was boulder-strewn, the ditches deep and quaggy, and we were driven half into them when a huge lumber truck with its heavy load of spruce logs went thundering by. The morning seemed far gone when ahead we saw the guides in dark clothes motioning toward our parking place. It was just ten.

The Club since the very beginning has been served by the fathers and sons of two Scottish families, long settled in the Maritimes, the Wayes and the Copps. Howard Copp was the head guide, Henry Waye, who was here to greet us, the head of transport: stocky, sandy-haired, with merry eyes, he helped stow our bags and duffle into his wagon which Morgan and Queen, a sturdy team, apparently immune to blackflies, as I was not, would haul over the tote road to Dam. We, traveling light with just our fishing gear, sweater, and toothbrush, followed Jack Waye over the ridges, through the wet meadows and along the corduroy that carried us the five miles to Stony Brook.

I simply made my bow to the camp, a well-stocked cabin set rather darkly in the trees, I had eyes only for the glorious salmon pool, wide and deep at the head, then curving and narrowing for some seventy yards along a rocky ledge to a dark overhung depth at the tail. "Water's pretty low," said Jim. "Doubt we'll do any business. Weeksie, you begin here and take it slow." "Here" was a stand without any entanglements at my back where I could get a good quartering drift across the current. "Remember," he called back over his shoulder, "don't try for too much, and once your fly is in, don't touch your line; let it ride." I felt very much alone when they'd left, unaware that a young guide setting out the luncheon was keeping an eye on me from the cabin. Unaware, too, that I was under another gaze. I made my way slowly, casting not very artfully and in silence. Across the water on which I was concentrating and to my left rear was a steep cliff from which, when he could tolerate no more, rose an eagle. For an instant he was over me with wings which to my terrified gaze seemed ten feet in spread. Then, dropping his compliments, he proceeded downstream. I had never been so close to a bird that size before and it took me a while to recover.

In any trio there will be one authority and Jim was ours. We deferred to him not only as our host but as the one who knew best, and I in particular tried to emulate his

bland, unhurried manner as he took command of a pool. We all drew a blank both in the forenoon and again after supper, confirming the hope that the best was still to come at Dam. "Bad luck to win the first hand," said Jim, who is a veteran poker player. Yes, but one day of the five had gone.

As the head of our party Jim had Howard Copp for his guide. Howard is a big man, broad-shouldered and wide-hipped, so big that there is the suggestion of the pachyderm as he tirelessly trudges the trail, and when he is casting, the rod looks like a wand in his hand. At first encounter it was his eyes I remembered, gentle and thoughtful, like his slow smile they gave the touch of beauty to his large head with its craggy features. He had a courtliness and a vocabulary that might have been Elizabethan. "In this hot weather," he would say, "the fish are dilatory." In the years to come we would all be the richer for Howard's philosophy of the woods. At this first stage I could see that he was kingpin and that the river where he had been a guide since he was sixteen was as close to his heart as his well-kept farm back in Red Bank.

"This trail," said Jim as he led the way next morning, "is the one the early members used back in the 1890's. It's quite a way, but we won't push it and we should pick up something at the Falls." As we filed along, from my place in the rear I kept hearing snatches of the argument about Dave's rod. Dave, who is thick-set with a strong torso, had been taught to fish by his father in Oregon and had beached his first steelhead, a 6-pounder, when he was twelve. But he had yet to tangle with an Atlantic salmon and now with a stubbornness that is part of his Scotch heritage he was maintaining that his Thomas trout-rod would be all he needed. "You can hold a fish with it all right," remonstrated Jim, "but it will take you half the morning to reel him in. The longer a salmon fights the less chance you have to bring him to the net."

"Well, we'll see," said Dave.

At the Falls, where powerful white water makes a swirling descent into scattered pools, with two good stands, Dave put the Thomas to the test and on the third cast was into a fish; it leapt quickly as grilse will, a bright fish who made one long run, and then the line went slack. "Damn," said Dave. "Lost him. But you see, Jimmie . . ." "Yes," said Jim, "but that was a grilse."

Now it was my turn. Clark Hare, my guide, the youngest and friskiest, tied on one of my Green Highlanders and cautioned me against letting it strike the rocks. I got plenty of advice about keeping my back cast high and felt momentary triumph when something struck and the line cut sharp diagonals. "It's a trout," said Clark, before I had seen it, which it was, beautifully colored and larger than any I'd ever netted at home. "Not worth bothering with," he remarked as he tossed it back in the stream. I swallowed my chagrin and now it was Jimmie's turn, but we had churned up the water and he drew a blank.

We "biled the kittle" at the Falls: strong black tea, ham and mustard on thick slices of homemade bread, toasted on the embers, sardines for a second, and ginger cookies. Then we went over the falls on a dizzying bridge of single logs which trembled to our weight, the white water rushing underfoot, our eyes and mind concentrated on keeping one's balance for the next step. We never looked up until we were across when we found ourselves at the foot of what neither Dave nor I had perceived, a flight of wooden treads, some forty of them, leading breathlessly up the cliff to a high plateau. "Thought I wouldn't spoil your lunch," grinned Jim. "Look where you put your feet and catch your breath at the landings." Under that blazing Canada sun even the guides lost some lard in the climb. Then we chewed the cud on a long hike across the uplands and descended through the warm breathing spruce until we came at last to the swift blue pools of Dam Camp.

Picture a house of one large room, thirty feet square and twenty feet high, firmly set on a crag twenty-five feet from a waterfall and some forty feet above Corner Pool into which the Falls plunge with the force of a fire hose. Within are a Franklin stove and huge woodbox, and hanging

from the rafters a handy pole-frame for drying clothes; a center table and comfortable chairs within easy reach of the drinks shelf; a photograph of the founding fathers dining solemnly in white ties at Delmonico's in 1899, and, in each corner, an iron cot with Hudson Bay blankets topped by a mosquito net for protection against those idiots who always leave the screen door open. The room is girdled on three sides by a covered porch with steep-pitched roof; it wears a cupola whose windows catch the breeze on hot days and the whole had been painted white with that same red trim I noticed on the forest gate. Windows open and the sound of the water always in your ears, not a murmur but a rushing. I was to wake very early at Dam, the water calling me to action by 3:30 or 4:00 A.M., and by the time my sneaker was casting its shadow on the floor I was impatient to go fishing. But when I shook Jim's shoulder he demurred. "Weeksie," he said drowsily, "go back to bed. You're bilin' the kittle at both ends."

When the guides open the camp each spring the clean snow is shovelled tight into the Snow House which becomes the repository for our viands and green fish and the source of snow-ice for cocktails. Balsam needles are scattered through the snow and give the martinis a unique flavor. The evening of our arrival we had drinks on the porch overlooking the falls while Jim explained the regime: "Breakfast at eight and we fish till noon when the guides like to be back in camp, unless you're taking your lunch upriver. In the afternoons we rest the pools and take naps and we fish again after supper till it's dark. We have two and a half miles of water to divide three ways — the Ledges and the upper pools; the home pools; and Black Pool and Mountain Brook below camp. Now, let's draw lots."

Jim and I shared the home pools for the first setting-forth and Dave went downriver. Clark stationed me on the rocky shelf midway in Basin Pool, an S curve of jet dark water, hurrying between walls of rocks with the tail of the S emptying into the eighty-yard open stretch of Basin Run. At its narrowest the pool is hardly fifteen yards across, though plenty deep, and I started stripping out line for a cast that would reach the other side. "Wait," said Clark, "first try the water that's handy. Here, let me show you." Taking the rod he reeled in until he had only two feet more than my leader and the fly. "Now," he said, "let the fly sink and work it slowly," his straight arm becoming part of the rod, "this way and that, this way and that . . ." Wham! The tip went down, the reel chattered, and he gave whatever it was the butt, setting the hook. "Here, take it," he said, handing me the rod and going for the net. Whatever it was stayed down for minutes, the line moving slightly; then a salmon shot clear out of water and as I watched, transfixed, turned a back cartwheel, thrashing with his tail, turned a second, still thrashing and was gone. "Should have lowered your tip," said Clark. "Good fish. With that tight a line he could knock it loose with his tail." Silence, while I trembled. "Likely he'll jump again to show he's free. . . . See, there!" So it was entered in the log that night that Weeks had lost a good salmon in Basin.

Next morning it was Dave's turn at the same spot and mine to go downriver but I lingered to watch him begin. On the top of the jutting cliff, below which Dave was casting, the slender spruce gave protective coloration for a lookout and here, Henry Waye, Dave's guide, was trying to spot the waving tail or shadow of a salmon beneath the dark panes of water. This would be easier when the sunlight invaded the little canyon, easier too, for the fish to detect the flash of the rod and the leader passing close to them. Dave, using a backhand cast, was covering the deep water effectively and we could follow the arc of the Black Dose. When nothing rose for it he changed to a Silver Grey, and still drew a blank. "Dave," I called down, "show me how you backhand a dry fly."

"Want me to? Well, it may be too early but why not."

The pool rested while he tied on a big Brown Wulff, gave it a touch of dressing and began to demonstrate. I noticed that he moved forward on the rocky shelf to get away from the back wall and that his backhand retrieve, which he turned his head to watch, sailed out over the water instead of coming close to the cliff. Looking back and following his wrist forward, he set a graceful rhythm which left the Brown Wulff riding slowly across the still water, at first close to us, then deeper and deeper in the gut. Without warning the fly was sucked under. Dave struck and the trout rod shook alive. "Weeksie," he cried, "I've got your fish!"

My fish or another, it shot out the gut and downstream into the open water, taking out line and the backing for what seemed close to a hundred yards. At the end of the run it jumped, and it was, unquestionably, a salmon.

"Clark and I are going to have to pass the rod to you," said Henry, "around this rock and down to the lower landing in the Run. Get there fast, Mr. McCord."

Dave handed over the rod, scrabbled up the rockface, raced through the trees and panted down the flight of wooden steps to a flat rock by the water's edge; I was following and I swear there were drops of his sweat on the wood. Clark, his left hand grappled to the base of a hemlock, swung toward us, relaying the rod to Dave's outstretched hand. The heavy tautness showed that the fish was still on.

Dave took in line when he could, then the fish would check, go off on a tangent, the light rod would bow down and we were back where he started. This went on for a long time. It was a weary triumph when Dave at last reeled in all the backing and his brown line began to show. Now the problem was to keep the fish from rubbing the leader against the half-submerged boulder in midstream: this was a new phase and it went on for a long time. (Yes, and I was supposed to be fishing.) The diagonal runs became shorter, the white of the salmon's belly began to show and at the end he came in a straight line almost gratefully to the net. We all shouted our relief and as Henry lifted him out and applied the priest — a stout chunk of spruce — between the eyes to still the quivering fish, I saw Dave turn his head away, with a little shiver of his shoulders. The death of a fine fighter; but the mood quickly shifted into a replay of the passing of the rod and general admiration for the prize. They were carrying him to the snow house as Clark and I went to our pools. I suspected — and I was right — that Dave would be borrowing Jim's spare salmon rod from now on.

I liked Clark, who was as eager and avid to fish as I. He wore his broad-brimmed felt at a rakish angle and he was very sure of himself on the rocks. We confided to each other as sports and guides will, each trying to get a picture of the other's life and though he realized that our tally would not make us top rod — a matter of secret pride to the guides — he was out to make a brave showing. On this my third day I killed a grilse that leapt eight times in the icy water that flows into the river from Mountain Brook; pricked something heavier in the shadow of the great tree, and hooked and lost another grilse. "If a salmon fought, pound for pound, as hard as grilse," said Clark, "there'd be no tackle to hold him." I also lost two flies and so much of my leader in the trees that at day's end Jim offered to tie on what he called a "tippet" of surgical gut, which I was glad to have him do.

On the morning before our departure Clark and I went upriver. At the Ledges I added a second grilse to my score which Clark hid in a rocky pool, covered with wet fern. "Plenty of grilse here but we're out for salmon. Let's go on to the Bulkheads. We'll be late for dinner but nobody's fished them."

It was hot, and I remember that the sweet scent of salmon emanated from Clark's net. We were dripping from the high going over the Ledges by the time we reached the Lower Bulkhead, and there Clark removed his shoes and socks, rolled up his pants, and, tiptoeing, began to reconnoiter, being careful to cast no shadow. This pool has a deep white-water throat which broadens and slows over sunken boulders; there are big spruce at the head and a wall of them to cast shadow on the northern bank. Suddenly, like Pavlova, with one leg suspended, Clark froze; then, so delicately as not to cause the slightest ripple, he returned to our bank to say that he'd spotted five large salmon lying in the shade at the outlet. Salmon, no grilse. It

would be a long cast. "Here," I said, handing him the rod, "you take the first crack while I get my shoes off." I watched him as I peeled. The long line shot out and the fly made its slow arc; then, at a commotion, it tightened; I saw Clark set the hook with the power of his forearm — and the leader broke. Knee-deep, he looked up at me with accusing eyes. "Clarkie, I didn't tie the damn thing!" I cried. I reached for my last new Hardy gut. Well, we soaked it for ten minutes, smoked, tied on my other Black Dose, and with bare feet I inched out along the sharp, slippery rocks to get within range. My first cast was short. "More line," said Clark, who was spying from the bluff. This will be it, I thought, and it was. When the white belly began to show and at last the spent, silver body came into the net, we let out that involuntary shout.

While we rested the pool, we argued over who would go next. "Try one more," insisted Clark. No angler ever quite repeats his performance, and certainly no beginner. As I edged back into the pool, I paused short of my initial position. Rocks were hard on my feet. The line was heavily wet now and hard to pick up. "Give her the gun," said Clark. I stripped off more line, swung the retrieve back, and started my forward lunge. There was an immovable tightness, a crack! — and I was left holding half a rod, the fly high in the spruce at my back. Silence as I reeled in and looked sheepishly at my mentor. "The middle section," he said, as he explored the break. "I think I could refit it over a fire, but it will take time." "Clarkie," I said, "we've had it. Let's go home."

Our last evening in camp we sat, leg-weary and relaxed, swatting the mosquitoes as Jim wrote up the log in that clear, telling script of his. Jim himself was top rod as he deserved to be and his 12-pounder taken from Corner Pool was the heaviest. My total of 1 salmon, 3 grilse, and several misses, was thought not too bad for a novice. And Dave had accepted that a salmon rod was for salmon. Our fish, so delicately smoked by Howard, would go out with us on the morrow. As Jim was pouring a dividend we all heard the plaintive call of the white-throated sparrow, the song so expressive of the north woods. We rarely saw the singer but listening to those far-carrying notes on the trail had put Dave's mind to work on a quatrain and he now produced it on a scrap of yellow paper:

> *By ledge of cedar root and stone*
> *I hear the hidden bird unflown.*
> *Cathedral in his tree above*
> *The level of my river-love.*

"Good for you, Davie," said Jim. "That belongs in the log."

5. "EVERY CHANCE YOU GET"

I SEEMED to be living in a wider horizon, aware of antennae I had not used before, with a keener respect for the country and a latchkey that kept opening new friendships. Nor was I alone, for Fritzy and young Ted were partners in this enterprise.

From mid-June, when Ted's school was over, to mid-

July was our favorite time for exploration. New England is at her greenest then, with the dew heavy on the morning grass and the wildflowers by the roadside so fresh as to invite the eye and slow the speedometer. In camp we early formed the habit of napping after lunch: this, in addition to resting the arm, gave us two days for every one, for when we awoke it was to a changing light and to that long-suspended silvery dusk that makes the evening pools so different from the morning.

We followed every lead, fishing for hatchery trout in the Norfolk Ponds and the Plymouth Reservation and bringing back our meager catch for supper that evening. We followed Henry Moore's column in the Boston *Herald* and when Henry reported that a large fish of salmon proportions had been seen leaping in the headwaters of the Parker River, down we pelted, Bobbie Livermore and I, with a canoe on the top of his car, and salmon rods which we set up on the side of Route 1A. We fished the banks, then launched upstream above the salt water line, casting the curves where the current made a natural pool: Bob recalled that Thomas Barbour and John Phillips, two Harvard naturalists, had introduced salmon fingerlings in the river as an experiment years before; perhaps a few of them had staggered their way home. He, not I, actually saw a big fish break water and taking turns we hopefully covered yard upon yard with different flies, and without a touch. Whether he was a salmon, a sturgeon — or the Loch Ness Monster — we shall never know.

In midsummer I bought a share in a syndicate owning a 15-foot skiff and a powerful outboard motor that could be throttled down for trolling. With an ex-paratrooper, Howard Wills, to guide us we went for all-day picnics in Ipswich Bay, trolling those tidal rivers, the Parker, the

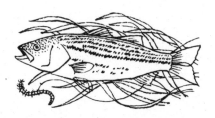

Rowley, and the Essex for school stripers. There is a saying that one must fish for one hundred hours for each striper taken, the truth of which we were out to prove. Howard had a quick eye for the shore birds and a dry humor. When Fritzy, caught short, looked yearningly at the out-house behind a shooting box on Rowley Point, and asked to be put ashore: "But what shall I do if there's someone in there?" she asked. "Just say, 'Push over!' " said Howard.

One night, trolling under a full moon with Shaw Mc-Kean, one of my partners in the syndicate, and Howard at the helm, I boated two 18-pounders in the channel off Castle Hill — "Well, I'm damned!" said Shaw — and later he picked up one of identical size at five the next morning at the mouth of the Rowley. That dawn we were the first to invade the night's quiet and from their resting place in the marsh grass three seal, gorged with fish, one after the other, lowered themselves into the stream and with baleful looks in our direction, disappeared.

These were the summers when that great-chested, great-hearted doctor, Wyman Richardson, was writing for the *Atlantic* those essays which capture the seasons of Cape Cod and that now compose his modest classic, *The House on Nauset Marsh*. Wy had carried three doctors' burdens during the war; his strength had been overtaxed and he was living on limited time. In what was to be his last summer he took Ted and me out in his long canoe to fish for school stripers in the Nauset Marsh and that evening his wife

Charlotte baked for our dinner a bigger one taken by young Henry from the Eastham surf. We had little cunners, fried crispy and tongue-hot, with our cocktails, and then the white-flaked bass with Char's special stuffing, and it was ambrosia. We sat talking of the elders who had loved this salt box in earlier times, Wyman's father and his uncle Frank Benson whose mural of the Canada goose in flight covered every wall of the living room. One of the geese was missing his neck and head. "My brother shot it off one night when he forgot he still had a shell in his gun," said Wyman. "Uncle Frank let the scar remain as a warning."

Food tastes better when you're on water. It always did in Sarge Kennedy's boat when with Peter and his wife and my associate editor, Charlie Morton, and Mildred, we cruised slowly of an evening off Crane's Beach and Wingaersheek. Charlie, not an angler, came along for the talk, the view, and the food of which he was a connoisseur. When supper could no longer be resisted we stood our rods in holders, and, still trolling, suspended operations. In one such pause, a fish defiantly hooked himself and in the scurry to get out of the way Charles stepped into the blueberry pie which incidentally was of his own making. It tasted just as good.

I early discovered that casting does not improve one's golf. In handling the fly rod the right arm is of course predominant (unless you are left-handed), indeed after a steady week of fishing it is easy to imagine that your right hand is generating twice the power of your left. On my return to the golf course after a spell of casting, I found it impossible to restrain my right hand, with some very sloppy results, either hooking or smothering my shots. This could be costly, and it was on my annual visits to Manchester, Vermont, to compete for the Flower Pot over the Memorial Day weekend. Henry C. Flower was our host and the foursome from Boston, George Batchelder, Joseph Spang, Richard Humphreys, and myself, were on our mettle to prove that we had the stamina, the hollow legs, and the putting touch to stand off the brigands whom Hank brought up with him from Manhattan. At the outset the Flower Pot was just what it sounds; a terra-cotta urn to hold our prize money and the penalty fees we had to contribute for anything worse than a 6 on the long testing seventh hole. Then Jack Herbert had the idea of converting the Pot into a silver replica of a thundermug; the silversmiths designed it with glee; and we played for a real trophy.

But at Manchester I thought I had the hardihood to wade the Battenkill in the morning and to play competitive golf through the long afternoons. The Battenkill in May is high, cold and powerful, and on one occasion when it had twice rolled me under I had such a fit of shakes in the afternoon that I could not sink even a six-inch putt. It is probably easier on your legs, and certainly easier on the pocketbook, if you elect to play one sport at a time.

I was always in a hurry at Manchester and usually being teased. The only one who did not taunt me was Duncan Read, a bird watcher, who would often accompany me along the riverbank. But even Dunc's loyalty dissolved in mirth on one woolly-headed morning. Hank, my host, had driven me to a remote stretch of the Battenkill with the promise to pick me up in three hours. Solitary and in waders I mounted my rod only to discover that having greased my line before breakfast I had left the reel back on my bureau. My struggle to locate a farmhouse with a telephone and then tell the taxi from Manchester where I was took time; the boys were down at the clubhouse when I reappeared and I hoped to steal in, retrieve the reel and get back to the stream unobserved. But Betty Flower spotted me, and the cat was out of the bag. Nowadays, like a forgetful housekeeper, I make a list of the essentials.

One other indulgence associated with fishing should be disposed of before I proceed to undiluted fly casting; I mean poker. I enjoy poker as much as any man but when I am trying to think like a salmon five hours of cards are too much of a distraction. Yet I must speak of one poker game which capped two days of trout fishing in Pennsylvania because the people involved were so pleasing. And the result.

I had been invited to receive an honorary degree and deliver the Commencement Address at the University of Pittsburgh. I suspected that my friend Edwin G. Peterson, one of the finest teachers of English composition in the East, was behind this and in all probability that he would write the citation. Peter is a first-class fisherman and when he suggested that we ought to fish together for a couple of days once our war paint had been removed, I was happy to agree.

I had heard of the reputation of the Loyalhanna, that small cold river which flows through the Rolling Rock country and those green wooded heights which are part of the Mellon domain, and it was a privilege, procured for us both by Leland Hazard and Lawrence Woods, to fish this lovely stream the evening after Commencement and all the next day. The river has been cultivated into a series of water terraces, boisterous at the deep end where the water flows over the individual dams and then slacking off into quieter shallows where the trout could be taken with a dry fly in the evening. There were some thirteen beats, the last passing under a bridge and into the main flow of the Loyal-hanna; from the bridge one could mark big chunky brown trout and over them the Professor and the Doctor of Letters worked with inward excitement but little to show for it.

We slept that night in the sumptuous quarters of the Rolling Rock Club, and having enjoyed how the other half lives, pushed on next morning into the old Indian country far to the north and west. Pete had just published his sumptuous book, *Penn's Woods,* in which are depicted in text and photograph those ancient and unsullied parts of the Commonwealth of Pennsylvania which still survive in a pristine state and now he was leading me to one of them, Spruce Creek.

He explained the setup as he drove. "Our host," he said, "is an able, self-made guy with a passion for this country. He has the local Chevrolet agency, acres and acres of fine farming country which his kids help him work, one of the oldest fieldstone houses in the county, and a lodge for guests on the edge of the creek. The beds are good, the refrigerator stuffed with steaks and fish and anything else you want, and there is only one requirement: that you play poker in the evening with our host and his sons."

Our host was immensely likable. He fished by himself, in secluded potholes, using worms and his trophies were a size and a half larger than ours. The poker game began promptly at eight and we closed out at midnight; present were our host, his two sons, the curator of the Indian museum, a traveling salesman, and myself. Pete did not take a hand; he had gone through his initial baptism, lost $30, and was excused thereafter. What we played was five-card stud, not with chips, but with silver and greenbacks. The limit was low but the raises rotated with such rapidity that I was almost dizzy, and the only way you could stop them after the last card was dealt was to plunk down $20, at which signal the others had to see you. I won one good hand; played close to the chest, and considered myself fortunate to be only $25 out at midnight.

All the next day we fished Spruce Creek. I came in for a drink of cold water in mid-morning just as a Junoesque daughter, tanned and in a dirndl, stopped by, got off her tractor, and came into the icebox for a Coke. She had evidently heard something about the man from Boston and may have been curious to see what he looked like.

The moon was coming up as we began our second night's play and the salesman had had a couple more drinks than previously. This time I could not miss. If my cards were low, they formed into two pairs and once a straight; if I had a queen down, another queen was sure to show up on the last card. All I had to do was ride with the raises and never quit. The pile of bills in front of me grew higher; our host began advising his sons when to stay out of the pot and arguing with them when they didn't; the salesman became fatalistic. At midnight when the game was over the host and I stepped out into the moonlight for one of those rare confidences which sometimes follow a bout of gambling.

"Brother," he said, "you were certainly shot with it tonight! . . . Listen, I want to tell you; I've been offered the chance at another agency. One of the boys and I could probably swing it in addition to what we are doing with the Chevvy, but I'd have to give up a lot of this. Do you think it would be worth it?"

"Lord, no," I replied, "you're sitting pretty with what you have. Keep it that way."

In our absence the kids had been counting my winnings and they totaled $127 and some silver. On my return to Boston it seemed to me the proper bread-and-butter was to send the landlord of Spruce Creek a two-year gift subscription to the *Atlantic*.

Walking home from the Club one winter's eve with Bob Cushman, who had just lost his son of college age, I remarked, unguardedly, that Ted and I were learning to use the fly rod together. "Do it," he said, and I felt the emotion in his voice. "Do it every chance you get. You have him with you so short a time."

For Ted's fifteenth birthday we gave him a lighter version of my rod, a shorter, more pliant Thomas; it matched his strength and how he cherished it! At this stage he was mostly long arms and legs and there were three parts of his fishing costume the eye could not miss: his hunting knife (never used) in a leather scabbard on his belt, his bulging fish bag which held every fly box and lure he treasured (and some I had, too), and his hat. Every angler puts a

superstitious trust in one hat. Ted's was khaki with a long visor with Polaroid glasses on the underside which like an outfielder he could flick down when he was scanning a stream. The top of the cap was studded with his old licenses, club emblems and a large "I Like Ike." They entrapped the branches when he ducked through the woods, and sometimes his line on a low backcast.

He was now in boarding school, Proctor Academy in northern New Hampshire, and to alleviate his spells of homesickness we drove up in the fall and early spring to take him out for the weekend. We tried our luck in the Blackwater — and very meager it was with the river so high — and nearly froze to death circling Lake Sunapee with the icy fingers of the north wind reaching right down our necks. The only good fish we saw was in the shallow water *under* the boathouse where I think he was huddling for warmth. Our favorite spot was Pleasant Lake and our favorite resort the lakeside cabin of Sidney Hayward's. Sid was the Secretary of Dartmouth College; he and his delightful wife Barbara had done their courting here when this was next door to wilderness and their cabin with its tiers of bunks had become a rallying point for Paul Sample, the artist in residence at Dartmouth, Corey Ford, the writer, and for privileged members of the Dartmouth Outing Club whom Sid would bring down with him on Saturdays. There was an old backwoodsman, Horace Turnbull, who came in to prepare Saturday night supper while we were still on the water — the crispiest, best-

seasoned corned beef hash I can remember and homemade apple pie. With that under your belt and the open fire radiating its untying warmth the yawns came soon.

Pleasant Lake is a small lovely body of water lying under the brow of Mount Kearsarge; it holds golden trout, landlocked salmon, some of considerable size, and native squaretails. Sid who had been familiar with the lake, dawn and dusk, for thirty-five years, knew where they were likely to be, and when. But the hardtop road brings aliens right to the water's edge and this water is hard hit, how hard we were to discover one Opening Day.

Opening Day in New Hampshire is traditionally May 1. We arrived in time to set up our rods, have the feast I have described, fill the thermos with hot coffee and set the clock for a five A.M. getaway. We needn't have bothered with the clock. Sometime before three, the first car rolled in with its trailer and the party launched the outboard, awakening the lakeside in their noisy advice to each other. Others kept coming until by five there was a putt-putting procession circling round and round the lake, counterclockwise, through a gathering blue haze of gasoline fumes. Any fish dumb enough to surface would have been struck dead by the drag of hardware these boats were towing. But none were: they just lay low and let nature take its course. By ten o'clock the fishing fleet was exhausted and, without a catch so far as I could see, they returned to the marina, hefted their boats back on the trailers and went away. An hour later when the breeze had dissipated the smog and

the sun had begun to warm the surface, Sid anchored us over a rocky shoal and at 11:10 the big trout began to come up, solid, black, brilliantly spotted, a pound to two pounds or better, they came to shrimp, to streamer flies, and to a silver squirrel tail of Sid's tying, the Hayward Special. There were three of us in the boat and we each had our limit when the great rise subsided in an hour. So did a few other weatherwise natives.

My stirrings toward Conservation (which up to this point had been concerned with distant objectives like the Redwoods or the Great Swamp in New Jersey) now began to focus on questions more personal and immediate, such as the silly saturation I had just witnessed. Was this a portent of how all roadside waters would be treated in the future? In my column in the *Atlantic* I had spoken my mind in defense of Walden Pond, Thoreau's old hermitage, which was always on the verge of being exploited, why not plead for the protection of clear-run streams, I thought to myself, and I began to do so. It would take me years to learn how difficult it is to keep any stream alive in the United States, and to this day I cannot understand why most Americans are contemptuous of the brooks, creeks, and rivers in their neighborhood, why they think running water is the proper repository for old bedsprings, dismantled cars, tin cans of all sizes, and any other unsightly, unwanted object. Yet "throw it in the crick" has been the family slogan since the colonies were a pup.

On our June trip north we always paused to look at the Bangor Pool, still to the eye one of the most picturesque, turbulent, and capacious salmon pools in the world. Before the pulp mills had contaminated the Penobscot, the Bangor Pool held hundreds, or if you go by the season, thousands, of bright salmon, and traditionally the first one killed each spring was packed in ice and sent to the White House. If one could find a fish there today, it would be half dead from lignen, the waste pouring out of paper mills forming an almost unbreakable solution of sulphuric acid. The industrial pollution which poisoned the lower waters of the Penobscot has had the same deadly effect on all the major rivers of the eastern seaboard, the Kennebec, the Merrimack, the Connecticut, to name but three, all of which were once famous for their salmon. Which is the chief reason why today American anglers head for Canada in the late spring.

The Northwest Miramichi, which I had tasted thanks to the hospitality of Jim White, and was to taste again, was still a little too rich for our blood and besides we lacked the necessary equipment; we hankered for something more modest in the north country and found it in Nova Scotia. In 1949 my friend Charlie Morton wrote an enchanting little piece for the *Atlantic* about the Milford House with its comfortable beds and fabulous cuisine, some sixteen miles from Annapolis Royal, and we were one of about forty *Atlantic* families who in the next years followed his advice and found it truly excellent. The main house with its dining room for all had an encircling brood of twenty-five log cabins, each with its own fireplace, hot water and private access to the lake. One could be as withdrawn or as gregarious as he pleased; we came for the fishing, not the cocktail parties, very early in June and virtually lived in our canoes.

The lake at South Milford is at the eastern end of a chain of waterways, inlets, and short portages leading mile upon mile into the interior, a flat uninhabited wet land, ruthlessly cut over early in this century but now densely shaded and thicketed by second growth. The trout fishing in the 1900's had been good enough for a book, *The Tent Dwellers,* by Albert Bigelow Paine; the abundance had been cut down since then, in part by the great deposits of sawdust the lumbermen had dumped in the streams which kept right on generating the lethal H_2SO_4 underwater for a radius of half a mile. But there were still wild trout and sturdy, moving about the lakes in schools and feeding, when the sun was hot, at the inflow of cold brooks. The problem was to find them and to guide us we had John, tall, dark and mild, who had been there as a boy when the Tent Dwellers were living under canvas and who had a charming way of coloring the present with the past. In fishing it is axiomatic that you always arrive too early or too late — "If you'd been here just after the ice went out . . ." they say, or "If you were only going to be here in September . . ." We were about forty years too late for the glory John recalled, but he kept feeding our hopes.

We averaged seven hours a day in the canoes, John and young Ted in the lead, Fritzy and I scuttling after, and for that length of time there are two portions of the anatomy which register special protests: it is hard for one's rump to find comfort in that narrow rattan seat, and for the last two hours of the seven, especially if you are paddling against the wind, you feel as if a hot iron was being ceaselessly pressed across the top of your shoulders. We always took the frypan with us and rarely caught more than we needed for lunch, and afterwards we all hunkered down and gave the back a rest.

We were the third guests to check in and the night after our arrival into the unfilled dining room walked E. B. White and his wife Katharine, that couple whose talents were so indispensable to the success of the *New Yorker.* (Their beloved hired man had just died of a heart attack and they had fled their farm in Blue Hill to assuage their grief.) In the lounge after supper we introduced ourselves and I added, "Ted, this is the author of your favorite book, *Stuart Little.*"

"Oh," said Ted. And then, after a pause: "But Mr. White, you must never do that again."

"Do what again, Ted?" asked the author.

"You must never let a character we've grown fond of drive right out of our lives the way Stuart does in his little car. I kept wanting him back." There were tears in his eyes as he said it.

After that I was known as the father of the critic.

John was over seventy and wanted to be home for his supper as much as I did for my martini, so we'd make an early start. The first two miles were always the same: some distance west from our landing we would slow down to cast the deeps under Pompey's Rock, draw the usual blank, then edge by the rock and into a new body of water; paddle by Battleship Island and turn left up the long corridor that led to Pike's Run. Here the speed of the water, the dense foliage, the streaks of sunlight piercing the trees all suggested mystery and monsters and John never let our hopes waver that at the Outlet where the cold water came out over deep rocks we would have the best fishing of the season, if we hit it right.

In the freshness of the morning family competition was hardly noticeable. Save for one precaution: since Fritzy had netted the largest trout last year, it seemed only fair that Ted and I should have the first casts over the untouched water until lunch. She accepted this in good grace except to dub me "the Admiral" and Ted "the Vice," which may have been her irony. When we had portages of any distance we beached one canoe, John took the lighter on his shoulders and we divided the pack, pots, ponchos, paddles, and rods, among ourselves. So we came to Thomas's Pool, in the early afternoon, not a breath on the water, four of us in the boat and John paddling so softly we barely moved. "Good pool," he whispered, "but best time to fish it is after dark. Then the big ones come out from underneath the banks." But only tiddlers came for us, barely enough for the frypan.

Over the canned peaches, cookies and John's thick black coffee ("That coffee is real able!" he used to say), I asked the question that had been growing in me, why in this vast uninhabited area had the supply of trout dropped so sharply since *The Tent Dwellers*. "Fall fishing, that's why!" said John with asperity. "Fifty years ago trout season ended in July, now they're working at 'em till middle of September. Take that Mrs. X up at the House, she won't even set in a canoe till September; says it's the only time to catch heavy fish. 'Course it is! She's draggin' in pregnant fish, stuffed with roe, so hungry they'd hit at a bit of flannel on a fork. You kill fish just before spawning time and you don't have so many fish to spawn. Stands to reason." It did.

John leaned back against a tree, lit a cigarette, and sighed. "Well," he reflected, "if I had a farm I'd sell it and go guiding." I was flat on my back, flexing my shoulders when out of the corner of my eye I saw Fritzy take Ted's light rod with the favorite killer, a little Parmachanee Belle, and move quietly toward the pool. Poor Ma, with those overhanging trees and blazing sun. "Watch your backcast," I murmured. Well, I'd better let her tell the rest of it as she did in the log that night:

Set out in a cold wind, red flannel underwear. First activity at Charlie's pool where, with great effort, 3 small fish were taken: 2 by the Admiral, 1 by the Vice Ad. Nothing more until the pool outside the lunch-ground stream [Thomas Brook]. There, four in one canoe, we hung up on the rocks while the Admiral snagged two medium sized, sporting chaps. Fished the big pool at the lunch ground with no sign of life. While John cooked lunch we went up the brook where the Admiral took 20¢ off the Vice Admiral by catching three (two legal length) in the riffles of the brook above. Late lunch: 2:30 to 3:30. At 3:30 my tale begins, innocently, with a small excursion on my own to the water's edge where I dabbled Teddie's Parma-Belle not trying for much because of trees at my back. *Socco!* a fish! When I recovered from the impact and decided I wasn't dreaming and saw that it was a fish & on to stay, I yelled for help. *Such* scurrying, and a netting problem since the terrain was like jelly under foot & my fish was within easy reach of the weeds. John solved the problem by having me walk the rod into the beached canoe where he followed me with the net. Operation successfully completed netting one thick trout 15¾ inches long. No more fish caught this day, but nice expedition, we all agree.

It was humiliating to have her get the biggest again, for we are reluctant to think her casting is all that superior.

Ted saved his congratulations until that night when she was tucking him in. "Ma," he said, "I didn't congratulate you but that was a great fish. But I wish you wouldn't always try to get the biggest. It makes it hard for me when I have to tell the boys at school." Yet she has her way of adding consolation as on the following day when, having caught my favorite blue fly in a high branch, I elected to mount from the canoe to a steep rock from which I hoped to tip down the branch. To reach the rock I had to edge in over the birch branches of a beaver house, a fussy business which made me impatient. As I got a firm footing with one sneaker on the rock, all unconsciously I thrust away with my retaining foot in the canoe. The further the canoe retreated the further I stretched until, rather than split, I dropped into the water and scrabbled for the rock. No word was spoken until I had salvaged the fly. Then, "With all that commotion," remarked the lady, "you shook down a dozen caterpillars. I wonder if a trout would take one." My wetness, stupidity, and barked knee were forgotten in the new possibility. She handed me one of the gray, silky blue-lined caterpillars, and from the tip of my paddle I dropped it in the run. It drifted twenty feet; there was a sudden smack and it was gone. The little things that count.

6. *THE PRESIDENTS IN THE GRANT*

MY road to Sidney Hayward's cabin on Pleasant Lake was to lead on to Hanover where in June 1950, and in company with other worthies I received an honorary degree from the hands of President John Dickey of Dartmouth. The Commencement exercises were held in a natural amphitheater, the Bema, and on the platform

I found myself seated beside a fellow editor, Harold Ross of the *New Yorker*. Ross sat with his mortarboard on his knees studying the program. "It says here," he remarked, "that I'm to be a Doctor of Humane Letters and that you're to be a Doctor of Literature. Must mean that I am a kinder man." "The hell it does," I exclaimed. "You turned me down for my first job the summer of 1923." At that moment Ross's name was called and he jammed the mortarboard on the back of his head and went forward to receive his citation.

When the ceremonies were over, we crossed the green-and-white elm-shaded campus to the President's house and in an aside during the buffet President Dickey gave me a tempting description of the Dartmouth Grant, the forest bounded by the Diamond River and just under the Canadian border, with which the state had initially endowed the College. "I'd like you to come up there and fish with me," said John — and that proved to be as happy an invitation as I have ever had.

One of the unpremeditated purposes of the Dartmouth Grant is to cool off the President after the rigor and festivities of Commencement. All Dartmouth Presidents are anglers — I assume it is a qualification for the job — but the two I have known should be classified as addicts. I never had the delight of fishing with President Hopkins, though we talked it whenever we met. But John Dickey has taken me up to the Grant for many a June and my love for the place and for the man has increased with each outing.

My anticipation begins to rise with the plane bearing me to West Lebanon, and as we taxi up to the gate of the little airport there is John looming above the waiting passengers with his rusty felt hat on the back of his head. I grin at the other members of the expedition, store my gear in the heavily laden beachwagon with the President's long green canoe strapped to the roof; John takes the wheel and we head north. John gives so much of himself to the double-barreled Commencement — first the seniors and parents, then the alumni — that it is no wonder if he is a little absent at the outset, like a house without its host. But this is the most beautiful drive in New England; we pass through the gleaming white hamlet of Orford, conjecture about the early days in those red brick mansions at Haverhill; catch water vistas such as that of the Connecticut at the Oxbow, and before we have reached the Salmon Pool on the Ammonoosuc, John's spirit has returned and the talk is flowing. On one of my early trips Dr. Jay Gile was with us, and his account of the buggy and sleigh rides he had made with his doctor-father through these same valleys half a century earlier peopled the road with a romance I have never forgotten.

We drive straight through with only a single stop to buy our licenses and the shadows are lengthening as we make the long run through the Thirteen Mile Woods with the pools and the white water of the Androscoggin showing through the spruce and hemlock. In our thoughts each man is already mounting his rod and trying to decide which fly, wet or dry, to begin with. But first there are two formalities: we make our politesse as we pass through the gate into the Grant. And then when at last we have reached the Management Center to be greeted by Bob Monahan, there is the succulent business of unloading. Mrs. Dickey never quite trusts our ability to net enough fish and so here in case of need are steaks the size of a catcher's mitt, homemade bread, a cherry pie, a tin of cookies, and a crock of fresh stewed rhubarb. Once they have been put in the icebox and the bunks dealt out, the President says in that drawl of his, "Well, I guess we might as well put up our rods and go to work." In his fishing shirt, rusty hat and waders, John at six feet four inches is a towering figure; he likes to wade and with his periscope advantage one can understand why. The Half Mile Falls have always challenged him, and after placing his guests on milder waters, this is probably where he will go.

For those who have never seen it, the Grant is a forest of 27,000 acres enclosed within the two spreading branches of the Diamond River, the Swift Diamond to the west, the Dead to the north. Eleven miles below Hell's Gate the streams flow together just before entering a roaring precipitous gorge. Along those eleven miles lives the forest which the College has been cutting and cultivating since 1807, an undetermined population of deer, bear, and varmints, and the wildest trout it has been my privilege to know. By preference we fish the Dead Diamond because it is the more navigable and because in its winding, wooded course it throws up sandy crescents with delectable pools at either end. The sand bears the footprints of wildlife but not a beer can, nor the chassis of an old Ford.

Those who have seen it will agree that the Grant is never the same. I have been there when it was so cold that my heavies and the layers of sweaters and windbreak were insufficient and other years when it was so hot that good fishing was confined to dusk and dawn. The hotter it gets the better the fishing and there never seems to be any shortage of black flies, mosquitoes, and no-see-ums. We fish in pairs, carrying a sandwich (mine always gets wet) and a chocolate bar. These we shove in with a handscoop of river water somewhere past the midpoint downstream, often at Slue Gundy, a deep pool still half in shadow at high noon.

On one occasion when John and I were working the upper stream and Sid Hayward and Paul Sample the lower, the wind came strong in our face as we approached the Slue. John, wading on ahead of me, put the full power of his right arm back of a dry fly oblivious to the fact that his back cast was already latched to an alder. The shock shivered his rod's middle joint but when I splashed in he had already improvised a splint made firm with adhesive tape and manila strands from the canoe's painter. With this contraption he hooked and was netting another trout, a scene which Paul has preserved in a watercolor.

Faces come out of the past. Sam, the Norwegian fire warden in his conical red hat, never removed, who fed the deer at his door in the dead of winter and who prefaced every one of his Paul Bunyan stories with "Pijesus, I vant to tell you . . ." Sid with his slow smile. Young John, now an able geologist but still in the Grant an appetizing and cheerful cook. John senior working away with a hammer and screwdriver to free the wedge of hamburg which he had stacked away in the ice compartment and had frozen solid. Dexter Keezer, the former president of Reed College, a master of the wet fly, bringing a sulking big fish to the surface; Dave McCord waxing poetic over a mug of rum; Beth Webster cooking scrambled eggs in the big skillet; George Harrar, president of the Rockefeller Foundation, reflectively wiping the dishes; Ralph Hill, the Vermont editor, discussing his plans for the new Dartmouth history, *The College on the Hill.*

And Sinclair Weeks, Secretary of Commerce under President Eisenhower. Sinclair is as staunch a Republican as I am a Democrat, and our trip in the tippiest of all canoes was conducted on a bipartisan policy until at the end we approached the logging bridge which crosses the

stream just above the Upper Farm landing. John was on
the bridge awaiting our arrival. I was in the bow in my
waders, Sinclair in the stern; the current was stronger
than either of us suspected, and as we neared the high bank
the canoe began to broach. "You can make it," said Sinny,
and I did, with a backward thrust of my left boot strong
enough to turn the canoe half over. "OH, NO!" cried John.
But Sinclair was more explicit. When we had got him back
to camp and dried him off, he denied that there were any
politics involved, but added, "You'd be a hell of a man on
the bridge of the *Queen Elizabeth!*"

Historically, the high point was President Eisenhower's
visit to the Grant in the spring of 1955. He had been visiting Sinclair Weeks in New Hampshire, and after deliver-
ing himself of half a dozen speeches, was on his way to
spend a fishing weekend at the Parmachanee Club in
Maine. John invited him to take lunch at the Grant on his
way east and with him came a retinue of senators, congress-
men, Secret Service men, and reporters. We who were
there to fish spent the day before the great event scouring
the river for a mess of trout. Sid Hayward and I made an
all-day foray on the Dead and with presidential privilege
each went beyond his limit, for we figured that we would
need a minimum of forty trout for those in the President's
party. It was warm work and the bugs were fierce. One
moose fly got me on the right temple when I was tied into
a strong fish and the welts there and behind both ears in-

vited scratching for several nights. Sam the fire warden, whose skin was impervious to any insect, went his own way downstream to the breakwater which checks the united river just before it enters the gorge. Here with worms he derricked up a perfect beauty, quite the largest, which was designated as "Ike's fish."

That Saturday there wasn't a cloud in the sky, and I remember that just after the gatehouse had telephoned to say that the cavalcade was coming in, a golden eagle, which had been nesting on the high cliffs across the valley, swung off and came drifting toward us riding the air currents, so John's greeting was, "Mr. President, there is an eagle up there which just came out to make you welcome," and as we all looked up, there he was.

As host that day John was perfection. Members of the Outing Club had come to camp the night before to cook a great pit of baked beans and to serve the trout. John presented every one of them individually to the great man, as he did Sam and the other wardens. It was an occasion when dignity and friendliness walked hand in hand.

The trout, all forty of them, were cooked on a bed of charcoal, so that they were done in an instant. But not "Ike's Fish." "That's not the way I want mine," he said. He asked for some chef's foil, rubbed down the beauty with a piece of bacon, added a touch of butter, then folded it in the foil and put it on the coals to bake. When it was unfolded he insisted that we each take a bite of it, and there was no question that it was the juiciest fish of the lot.

The President had no thought of fishing the Grant with a delegation from Congress and a score of reporters watching him from the bank, and in the early afternoon he moved on to Maine. Later that same evening after we had supped, a lumber truck pulled up in the yard and in came a stocky French Canadian reeking with liquor. We will call him Henri Ledur. He had been logging in the Grant and living there in a tarpaper cabin, drinking hard, impervious to Bob Monahan's warning, and when his jags were on him, beating his spunky little Indian wife. There and then in ten minutes of downright masculinity, John put him on the carpet, reducing him — temporarily — to repentance and sobriety. That man-to-man talk in the half-light was something to have heard; it too is part of the history.

In the aftermath it was amusing to compare the preparations which the three states had made for Ike. Vermont presented him with an Orvis fly rod but saw no necessity of offering him better luck than a casual visitor would have on Vermont water, and with his gift I believe Ike netted one trout. New Hampshire, where he made several short speeches, seeded the streams he was expected to fish with several "biggies" from the state hatcheries, but made no effort to fence them in. The waters of the Parmachanee Club in Maine, where Ike was planning to spend the week-end, were once famous for big trout which had now become rather sparse. So the Parmachanee pools were seeded for the great man with fish of size that were not exactly tethered, but shall we say, corraled, and here for half a day, until he found out about it, the President had good sport. But when he learned that the victims had been planted there and corraled for his benefit, he was furious. "It's no fun fishing in a prison," he exclaimed, and that kind of a party was over.

7. *THE GIFT OF THE RODS*

WATER was much more on my mind these days. I
was beginning to write about it and encourage others
to do so. The Army Engineers, who are just about a law
unto themselves, and the Bureau of Reclamation were filling the air with plans to dam this river or divert that one;
the mighty Missouri was lucky to escape with its life from
the grandiose schemes of General Pick, the public lands
and national parks were being molested and resentment

against all this was mounting among conservationists. I believed *Atlantic* readers were warming to this (even to my fishing), a feeling not always reciprocated by members of my staff who sought to restrain my zeal with the tag "Speckled Beauties." "Another piece on Speckled Beauties. One more than we need. No!" was the way they put it in their reports. They were overruled.

In August I began my "Peripatetic Reviewer" with these words: "Because I find fishing, the play of sunlight and shadow on water and the signals of the life beneath, the most complete and bewitching relaxation from a life devoted to print, I am occasionally asked for advice, not as an expert but as an addict who has learned from his trials . . ." That was my last out-of-doors piece of the season as I folded my rods early to prepare a new series of lectures for a Western tour which took me in late September to university campuses in Southern California and on to others as far north as Seattle.

On my return to Boston I noticed a narrow wooden coffin four feet high, standing conspicuously in the corner of my office. Express tags showed it had been sent by F. L. Smith of Beverly Hills; I couldn't remember meeting anyone of that name. "It's been here three days," said the secretaries, "but not a word about it. What the heck is it? Aren't you curious? "Sure, sure," I said, "but let me look at the mail first." No, they could hardly restrain themselves while I did. *"If* you take off the Express tag," I said, "you'll probably find a poem on the back." It was sheer guesswork but I was right. There underneath, handwritten, were these lines:

> *By fifty battling years unbent*
> *Proud of your honored name,—*
> *Wherever it is you now have went,*
> *I hope they'll be glad you've came!*

When the shipping room opened the box, it contained, as I had suspected it might, a long aluminum tube. Inside, carefully enfolded in green felt, was a Leonard trout rod, freshly varnished.

The mystery of the sender continued for another three weeks and was then resolved by this letter:

Beverly Hills, California
November 18, 1952

My dear Mr. Weeks:

For some time I have been endeavouring to get a letter off to you which might help to explain the recent shipment by express of an ancient fly rod, lacking which explanation it may have been a source of annoyance and almost certainly a matter of puzzlement. In writing you now, very belatedly, I am reminded of a large print copy of the sound advice as passed on by Matthew, being in fact, one of the lesser Beatitudes, which I kept on my office table in Detroit during a considerable period of time in which I was pestered by all manner of people wasting my time in trying to sell me what I did not want. The item reads, "Let your communication be, Yea, yea; Nay, nay: for whatsoever is more than these cometh of evil." I know in advance that this present communication will be a mile or two away from following the sage advice of the late Matthew. I can assure you, however, that long or short, this communication needs no acknowledgement whatsoever, and that, my dear sir, parole d'honneur, is an empty figure of speech but one hundred per cent sincere.

The reason for writing you is to be found in the August issue of the *Atlantic*, wherein you furnish an answer to the question of why fishing seizes on us with a really gripping force. I also have been asked many times about this and that matter having to do with fishing and quite often what it is that leads one to take it up as a hobby and to ride that hobby for all his life. If the question is ever again put to me I shall bow my head as one sunk in deep meditation and finally come up with this in my mouth, "I find fishing, the play of sunlight and shadow on water and the signals of the life beneath, the most complete and bewitching relaxation from a life devoted to . . ." Devoted to tending to other people's business, in my case. After searching my soul for at least half a century for words to express what fishing is, you have given me the perfect answer in three short lines. Those are lovely portmanteau words that not even Humpty Dumpty could have equalled, and I am now writing to express my gratitude.

As to the rod, that was a shot in the dark but I assure you if it has no interest at all for you or for someone that you think might use it, that will be quite all right for me. It was, and I think still is, a sweet little rod and if it is again put to active service and goes bust, that also will be quite OK. The metal tube, I was lucky to find and The Boss tailored a new cloth case for Leonardo. Both of us hope that some use may be found for it and both without the least regret because it was merely growing old in a dark corner, unwept, unhonored and unsung. Leonardo is something over fifty years old, just how much older I cannot precisely state. He has fished in too many places to list them here but roughly speaking from British Columbia to New Zealand and from New Brunswick to Bermuda and Trinidad. The Boss and I often go over what we have come to call Leonardo's Last Stand on the Waimana in New Zealand where we camped for a week at the very end of the very worst road in all the world. It is too long a tale to indulge in now but it has to do with a battle with a six and one-half pound rainbow trout in fast water; the battle being witnessed by The Boss and our guide who both swear that in making a series of spectacular leaps, the fish went clear to the bottom of the pool to get leverage for his tail before he shot up, I do not dare say how many feet into the air.

The autobiography of The Boss and your present cor-

respondent, I think I can make commendably brief. We have fished pretty well up and down the Atlantic and Pacific and for all kinds of sporting fish. We gave up deep sea fishing some years back as being too strenuous and not half as sporting as using light tackle on salmon, trout and small-mouthed bass. For trout fishing, South Island of New Zealand is easily in the top bracket. We have never fished at Cascopedia but have fished year after year the one and only Restigouche, with the final comment that salmon fishing on the West Coast rates the low bracket by comparison and it looks at present as though our fishing days were regretfully a thing of the past.

To revert to your "piece" in the *Atlantic*, an added reason for making you a target for this barrage was your reference to your "lovely Thomas rod," the more by token that The Boss and I, over a period of years have amassed, so to speak, six Thomas Brown Tones, including two two-piece Gems which were to me a revolution in fly rods. That looks like a plutocratic boast, meaning the possession of six Thomas rods, but it was spread over a period of years and made necessary by the fact that some of our family and some of our guests could not be expected to make the grade for one trip only. I neglected to say that the little rod sent to you was a special order executed, I was told, by old man Leonard himself. The tips weigh one-half ounce apiece and vary in length one inch from each other but the final weight of the whole rod ran over the estimate by nearly three quarters of an ounce due to the fact that Leonard suggested the laminated cork grip instead of the whipcord winding originally planned and also a trifle added weight occurred in the reel seat, the original intent being to bind the reel to the butt by strong but light linen line. I will also add that if you notice a slight aroma of ether when you open the rod case that comes from the gadget which I cemented to the top of the case as a buffer. It was my own invention being about as useless, I think, as those of our friend the White Knight.

In closing, if you wonder how I know that you are An Alice Addict, the answer is that you told me so yourself, many years ago, that time we exchanged amenities apropos of one of your highbrow contributors who grievously misquoted the beautiful poem wherein the small boy gets properly taken care of when he sneezes.

I think this will be all for today and, once more, you have brought it all upon your own head by your own perfect handling of the Fishing Definition.

Very truly yours,
FRED L. SMITH

I had received fan mail for my articles and broadcasts but nothing that touched me as this did. I wrote our gratitude to Mr. Smith telling him of how close I had come to his home when he was in the act of making me the present and of the fun we had on our family trips to Nova Scotia — for which we would now be equipped!

(I told my friend John Mason Brown about Leonardo at the time when the charges against Major General Harry Vaughan, one of President Truman's assistants, were in fresh memory. John looked at me sagely. "Ted," he said, "if you wrote another column, do you suppose you could get yourself a Cadillac and me a Deepfreeze?")

I suppose I should have been warned by the clue in Mr. Smith's letter as to what would follow, but I was not. My birthday is the 19th of February and the day before it in came a larger coffin, almost as tall as myself, and from the same donor, this one containing two salmon rods, the two-piece Thomases he wrote about, his with his initials on the

canvas jacket, weighing 7⅝ ounces; the Boss's a replica only a little lighter, 7⅜. Accompanying them were two Hardy reels with silk lines to balance. I set up the rods in our living room after my birthday dinner and we took turns flicking them, and feeling them tremble with the eagerness the Smiths, bless them, had transmitted to us.

I was never to meet our benefactor but I am sensitive to his generosity every time I take the rods out of their cases; I wrote to tell him how and where we were using them until his death, and thereafter to "The Boss."

8. *THE ENGLISH EXPOSURE*

A T the end of the Second World War, when the new
transatlantic planes made the flight to Europe so
much more comfortably than the old flying boats, I planned
on an annual visit to England to scout for articles and authors. Someone told me that the month of April has the
highest incidence of sunlight in the British calendar, so I
came then and stayed until early May, tasting their spring

before I returned to ours. I took with me a trout rod, and a set of waders with heavy underwear which I checked in my London hotel at the end of each visit. This proved to be opportune, and in time the same rod went with me on speaking trips to California and on my "cultural" visits to the Soviet Union and to Yugoslavia.

Edward R. Hewitt, the Aristotle of American anglers, had a number of magnificent prejudices which, given an audience, he would proceed to harp on at length, and one of them was his distrust of the British diet, which in his view had in it more than enough starch to deplete the Empire-builders. Well, I confess I had my own troubles with the London menu, which left me feeling like a snake that had swallowed a tennis ball, but this surfeit was due to an excess of hospitality. When I arrived I was asked the traditional question by my friends in the publishing houses and literary agencies: "Are you here for pleasure or here to read?" I was there to read, and my wife too on many occasions and in no time our suite at the Stafford would be heaped with galley proofs and advance copies of English books still needing an American sponsor, and with shorter manuscripts for the *Atlantic* from diverse sources, also four daily newspapers and all the weeklies including *Punch*. For a visiting editor the London regime admits of at least five opportunities for the giving and receiving of food and drink: breakfast, lunch, tea, drinks (6:00–7:30 P.M.), and dinner or supper, either before or after the theater. The closer one comes to departure the more they all are utilized, and the impact on the digestive system is terrific.

I doubt I should have survived without the antidote of my fly rod. Each week from Monday on I was seeing people, talking, persuading, reading or listening until Friday afternoon when, talked out and jaded, I had thoughts only for the country, simple food, a stream and a comfortable friend who would not mind my distraction.

The first author to be my fishing companion was Geoffrey Household. Geoff is a master of suspense in fiction, and his many fine short stories which we featured in the *Atlantic* and novels such as *Rogue Male* and *Watcher in the Shadows* put him on a par with John Buchan and have all eventually been published in book form under the Atlantic–Little, Brown imprint. Although he has worked everywhere, as a bank clerk in Bucharest, selling ink in Latin America, as an infantry officer in Greece, and on mysterious missions in the Levant later in the war, Geoff is first and last a countryman whose ruddy complexion, trim figure, close-cropped mustache and general air of command are the portrait of a Brigadier. At war's end he, Ilona, his Hungarian-born wife, and their children went to live with Geoff's father in an old schoolhouse in Dorset, close by the Thomas Hardy country, and here while England was still on short rations we came to visit. From Canada I had airmailed a rib roast and a steak timed for our arrival Easter weekend, and little Nyusi, the nine-year-old son who had never seen that much of a steer and had been told it was flying over from America, kept looking anxiously up in the sky for it to appear.

Fishing is not in Geoff's book but he had wangled permission for me to try his neighbor's brook on Saturday afternoon and he and Nyusi came along for the sport. There wasn't any. Green as I was to the habits of the brown trout, I fished all the wrong places, the open water instead of letting my fly ride over the dark submerged grass, and we came away with an empty creel. As we trudged home across the meadows, all thoughts of a trout supper gone glimmering, I can still hear Nyusi's little treble saying,

"Papa, Mr. Weeks must be a wretched fisherman, not to catch even one." But in our absence the beef had arrived and I was excused.

Easter morning, and a cold one, we attended service and early afternoon when we set out for the river Piddle a cutting wind was blustering down from the north. Geoff had secured a two-day permission for me to fish Sir Ernest Debenham's waters lying — I remember the quaint wording — "between the village of Puddleton and the Chamberlain's boundary." We first paid our respects to Sir Ernest, an octogenarian, who made us welcome and presented me with a little blue permit book, stipulating among other things: "Dry fly only; no wading whatever; First Brace for the master; thereafter an even division until the limit of four brace have been taken." White-haired and hearty, he led me to the big window where from his couch he could see the lovely, curving course of the chalk stream, every pool of which held memories. "The fish should be in prime condition," he said. "A March Brown is all you need, and be sure to fish the center of the stream. My bailiff will show you to the good water. I wish I could join you!"

It was so cold the girls stayed in the car, but Geoff and Nyusi, with his bare legs, insisted on watching, huddled in the lee of some blackthorn. So, after a bit, did a young couple who stopped their motorbike near the bridge while I was netting. Things happened so fast that I fought the wind instinctively, changed flies only when the first became waterlogged, and in little over an hour when we were again at Sir Ernest's door, I asked the butler for a platter and on it presented to the master my largest trout, which was just under three pounds. "God bless us!" he said, "your limit in that space of time!" and his delight was as warming as his sherry and the open fire.

From the Stafford Hotel it is but a few steps to St. James's, the street I most relish in London. Here is every delight but one to please the male: wine from Berry Brothers, whose cellars deep under the pavement were first reinforced to support the coronation coaches of Charles II; hats from Lock's, whose shop has been swept but otherwise unchanged from the days they were shaping a cocked hat for Lord Nelson; from Prunier's delectable bisque homard and Dover sole; from Webley's a fowling piece or rifle to match your build, and at the upper level, those clubs, Boodle's and White's, Brooks's and Pratt's, whose banter and decorum are a perpetual surprise to the American visitor. Around the lower end of St. James's on Pall Mall and across from the Palace is Hardy's Fishing. Hardy's is the cornucopia of English angling; the shop is run with a quiet air of authority and it has everything: the long rods the English prefer and need for their streams; flies from the tiniest, exquisitely tinted drys to the big Salmon flies for heavy water, as large as the bowl of a serving spoon but much more deadly; nets and leaders (in England "casts"), the latest word in fishing hats and waterproofs — everything, including good advice proffered by the clerks in their dark clothes required for town wear. One of the most considerate of them all was Mr. Beauchamp, who became my tutor.

I got him to pick out an assortment of dry flies such as he himself might use on the chalk streams and to write their names in his precise script in the little square on the inside cover of the fly box, and approximately in the order that I might need them as the day advanced, beginning with the Iron Blue and Gray Olive, passing on to Lunn's Particular

("Good anytime, that one, sir"), and coming down to the late evening flies, the Orange Sedge and the Houghton Ruby.

I could not spend every Easter with the Households and since few of my publishing friends would be in their offices from Maundy Thursday until the Tuesday after, it seemed to me on my next trip that here was a heaven-sent opportunity for a fishing adventure on my own, and I asked Mr. Beauchamp where to go. He consulted the big ledger in which Hardy records the latest news from the most fishable streams from the north of Scotland to Land's End, and then recommended the River Tamar in South Devon. "The salmon should be running at this time of year," he said. "There are plenty of trout in those waters and if there's a room for you in the Arundel Arms, you will be comfortable indeed." I telephoned the inn to ask for reservations for four and then I telephoned my oldest friend in England, H. R. Creswick, with whom I had shared rooms in Great Court, Trinity, in 1922–23. Dick as an undergraduate was interested in rare books which he purchased from Old David, the secondhand bookseller in the Market Place; it was a lifelong interest which led him on to be Director of the Bodleian, Oxford, and then for twenty years Director of the University Library, Cambridge, the only bookman in history to achieve both offices. We spoke the same language.

"Dick," I said, "I've got some trout fishing reserved for us down in Devon for the long Easter weekend. Do say you and Agnes can join us!"

He seemed slightly incredulous but willing, and in the upshot we joined them in Cambridge and motored down, pausing to pay our respects to the rustic beauty of Stratford and Broadway, and pausing again to stretch our legs and take early tea at Bath. Motoring with Dick is not an endless race as it is on our American throughways; the bookman in him keeps looking for signs of the past and in Bath we found them in the Roman remains which put me in mind of Kipling's story "A Centurion of the Thirtieth." ("Dick," I asked, "how do you think they reacted here when they heard that Rome had been sacked and that no more legions could be spared for Roman Britain?"); we also found something of the more graceful past in those immaculate crescents which we tried to people as in Beau Nash's day. With one thing and another we reached the Arundel Arms in the tiny hilly hamlet of Lifton barely in time for sherry and dinner.

This was my first experience at a fishing inn and I was much taken with it. The Arms and the water on the three streams it controlled were the property of a benign manufacturer of powdered milk; he liked fishing and reserved for himself certain salmon pools; he also liked eating, and his chef at the Inn had a reputation for roast chicken with skin that crackled, Yorkshire pudding as light as a popover and crème brulière of which Trinity College would be proud.

After a day on the Tamar and its tributaries the guests assembled to compare notes over drinks before dinner; the catch, brown trout and occasionally a salmon, were displayed on a vast platter (they would later be iced and sold by the inn), and after the meal, without apparent haste or greed, the anglers signed up in the Book for the beats they would fish on the morrow. You could not hold on, day after day — or even every second day — to the more desirable stretches; it was reasoned that those here for a long stay would have their share and that the brief-comers should be given fair chance. Threading his way through the banter

and recitals was a quiet-spoken colonel (ret.) who super-
vised the fishing and had flies or boots for those in need.
Dick and I turned to him for tips as the water was exceptionally high and we wanted to know where the trout would
best respond to the dry fly ("The slow run behind the
schoolhouse," he said) and where I should try my salmon
rod. Dick was fishing only for trout.

For my first day I drew a rather deep stretch at such a
distance from the inn that we took with us what the Colonel
called "a packed lunch." Dick drove us to a little lane
sunken between blackthorn in bloom which finally became
so narrow the car couldn't pass; here he left us saying he'd
be back at five o'clock, and I entered the stream by the small
white stake which bounded my domain, with Fritzy, loaded
with lunch and camera, trailing along above me on the
bank. As we approached the railroad bridge there seemed
to be a good shaded run close to the left: I inched my way,
working up to the dark water under the bridge in short
quartering casts; one moment I was wading waist-deep, the
next there was nothing to tread on and I quietly, coldly
submerged. Watching from above, Fritzy saw me sink until
only my hat was above the surface; undecided, torn between the impulse to photograph and the apprehension that
she might have to plunge in, she was relieved when the hat

began to rise and I under it as my boots caught hold of the
bottom the other side of a deep hole. Breathless and damp
from the shoulders down I squelched up the bank. It was
much too far to think of walking to the Inn in wet boots so
I stripped, wrung out my heavies and let the April wind
and what *The Times* in its forecasts refers to as "an occasional bright interval" dry me and my garments. The
cows in the next meadow were unconcerned, there was no
one else in sight and what with Fritzy's hoots and a nip of
Scotch I was back in action in an hour and quite dry by
noon. "I meant to warn you about that hole," said the
Colonel when I told him that evening. "Actually there are
two of them, made when the bridge was built — which did
you choose?"

Dick got our best fish that year and a fine sight it was on
the white platter. Time flies when spring days are as happy
as ours at Lifton and I still smile over one incident which
illustrates that English angling does not always run true to
form. It was understood that an angler lucky enough to
hook a salmon had the choice of bringing it to the net or
beaching it but under no circumstances should he use the
gaff, a stout pole with a sharp, wicked hook on the end.
Among the guests were a sprinkling of officers who had
retired after the war and the largest and ruddiest of whom
we nicknamed "the General," as he may well have been. He
was deferred to for his knowledge of the place and in his
bland way he expected and received certain privileges. In
my effort to lure a salmon I thought it sensible to follow
his choice of beats and one morning as I was casting a pool
in which the General said he had risen a salmon the day before I came on a weapon lying on the bank which brought
me to a halt. It was certainly a gaff but an outsize one,
more like a halberd that might have been borrowed from

the Tower of London. Any fish, fighting for its life, impaled on this would soon expire. At day's end I brought the trophy home and showed it to the Colonel.

"Yes," he said, "it belongs to the General. I'd return it to him but perhaps not at drinks." When I did so, the great man said simply, "Thank you, my dear boy."

I set no records on the Tamar; I think my finest moment came on the run behind the schoolhouse when at dusk, with the Colonel watching, some veteran trout, to judge by the size of the rings, began feeding hardly a foot from the opposite shore. I was well below them but my problem was complicated by the giant beech on either bank whose branches almost interlocked overhead: I had to make a side-arm cast to keep my fly out of the branches but with enough length so that it would drop above the rings, short of the bank, and drift languidly downstream. After some thirty false casts this happened: the little Orange Sedge rode placidly six inches from the bank; there was a roil, I waited, then cocked my wrist, felt the strength of the fish, and the leader broke. "Well done!" said the Colonel. "You had him well hooked. He was a good fish. Too bad."

What I began to learn in Devon — from the Colonel, if not from the General — was the etiquette of British angling. I was impressed by the respect which the Colonel and the guests both had for the beats they were fishing. There were no bottles or tin cans carelessly tossed into the stream, no fragments of a picnic shoved under a bush. I don't mean the riverbanks were manicured, simply that they were left in a state of nature. I was impressed by the absence of competition when the time came to select one's fishing for the next day. There must be fish hogs in England as there are in America, but I did not chance to meet them at the Arundel Arms. Finally, I was impressed by the nicety, even the elegance with which these people dressed for their fishing. Not for them the Sloppy Joe hats and greasy lumber shirts in which we throw off the tedium of business. The English in their hats, tweed jackets and waterproofs are professionally trim.

There is something to be said for the innocence of the eager. When I gave Mr. Beauchamp a grateful report of our trip to the Tamar I went on to ask whether there wasn't a trout stream closer to London which I might fish for a day or two at a time, the Test, for instance?

He looked at me gravely, "You're asking for the best chalk stream in Britain," he said. "But because you're an American they might just make an exception for you. Call up Miss Kay Potts at Leckford and throw yourself on her mercy." I did so only to be told that they were booked solid through June; then her voice relented, "If you care to come down for a single afternoon and evening on April 19th," she said, "I can put you on Beat 5. But I must warn you that the farmers will then be cutting the banks and the river will be heavy with vegetation." I blessed her for the chance and on the morning of the 19th took the two-hour train trip to Andover and a cross-country taxi to that glorious valley in Hampshire which is today the most cultivated school of fishing in the world. The pools I was being admitted to were directly upstream from those of the famous Houghton Club.

I checked in at the Leckford Abbas, bolted down a slice of fruit cake with my tea, said hello to Miss Potts, who was cordial and direct in her welcome as she told me where Mr. Mott, the head keeper, would meet me on the stream, and in my Wellingtons, down I clumped to Beat 5, a bundle of anticipation. The afternoon was cold and overcast, the downriver wind strong in my face and the water looked like the floating gardens of Babylon. The farmers had indeed been cutting and the problem was to drop a fly in the clear spaces between the drifting brush when a trout was rising. My beat consisted of a broad deep stretch of the Test and angling off from it some narrow, shallow canals known as "carriers."

"You're standing rather close to the water," said the quiet voice of Mr. Mott, a tall lean countryman with fine eyes, in his gray tweeds and cap, a friendly advisor I was to depend on in days to come. We shook hands, he looked approvingly at the Blue Upright which I had on my line and with disgust at the clotted stream. "When the river's clear," he said, "we stand or kneel well back of the bank so the fish won't see us. That means a high retrieve to keep the fly out of the rushes behind you — which is why we favor the longer rod." Then he stood by watching and I became more and more inept, as one does in the face of an expert. "Be sure to fish the carriers before dusk," he cautioned, with just a hint of encouragement before he turned away. When he had departed and I was convinced that this was one day the fish could not see me, I not only returned to the edge, I ran along it, dapping my fly in any available opening. Twice, at dusk, I had a fish on — but not for long. That was my first day.

I was, of course, being looked over and my eagerness if not my skill may have tipped the balance for Miss Potts

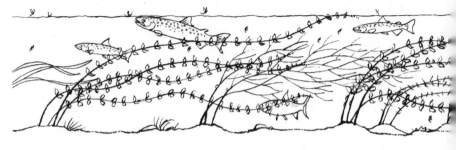

seemed genuinely sorry that she had no other beat to offer
when I paid my fee the following morning. "Well," I said,
facetiously, "I shall be praying that one of your members
will sprain an ankle while I am still in London. If that
does happen, Miss Potts, will you please be sure to telephone me? I shall be praying hard." That was on a Tuesday and on Friday morning a call came through. One of the
partners had gone off to the hospital for a checkup, releasing four days the first week in May. They were at my disposal. Conscience forbade my taking all, so I compromised
on two, Beat 8 for my first day and No. 3 for my second.

The conditions which were awaiting me a fortnight later
were quite different and more difficult. On my first morning
as I crossed over the little railroad bridge that led to the
top of my beat I paused to savor my surroundings. The
Test as it approaches the village of Stockbridge is a quick,
deep stream rarely wider than forty yards; it is controlled
by a system of weirs which keep the depth constant and the
water tumbling with life, while breaking off from the main
current are the narrow carriers, some as straight as a canal,
others curving away for half a mile through shaded banks
before they rejoin, forming succulent pools at their re-
entry. On this particular day the windows of the sun as
they opened through the high clouds lit up the whole valley
in different planes, the landmarks, the white chalk cliff,
the beechwoods, the steeple at Longstock being now in sun-

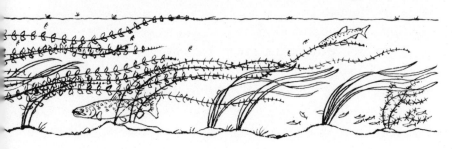

light, now in shadow. Ahead of me was the little thatched hut in which I would park my sandwiches and raingear, and beside the bridge waiting to greet me, Mr. Mott.

I had that blissful feeling of trout impending and the whole day ahead. Looking upstream Mr. Mott pointed to some of the hot spots: the deceptive quiet stretch to the right of the great willow, and the fine pools to the right and left of the point of the island, formed by the carrier; then turning about he studied the turbulent water below the bridge: "There are some very strong fish in this pool," he said. "See, there's one feeding now!" (Peering at the sun-points dancing on the fast water I could distinguish nothing.) "But it's not easy to fish — you have but a second or two before the fly is drowned. Best save it till dusk when the big ones drift down to the quiet end."

On my own I started up the left bank toward the willow where I could see a fish coming regularly to the surface. The hatch was on, flies were in the air and on the water, and I thought my Blue Upright a fair replica. The river was clear as a martini and the banks, now cut, were so damp and tremulous that even at three feet from the brink my tread sent fish arrowing into midstream. Brown trout seldom move far from their favorite lair unless fright sends them but once startled it will be some time before they resume their feeding ground. From then on I picked my way at the base of the high grass which seemed to have grown a foot in my absence.

By now fish were feeding up and downstream. I saw the big one by the willow, his green and silver perpendicular beauty as he rose close to the bank for my fly — and then saw me, or rather the drag in my line, and turned away. I was learning that the largest fish survive in the Test because they grow wary and because it is so darned difficult for duffers like myself to keep a fly from dragging or drowning in that powerful current. I began looking for more protected pockets.

The hatch is short-lived in the spring and I thought I was beginning to see a new batch, flies of a yellowish hue, so I changed to a Gray Olive and had three good strikes in the next twenty minutes, each one of which I missed.

Mr. Mott, who has the eyes of a falcon, had been watching from afar and now came up. "You've been striking too soon, Mr. Weeks," he said. "These browns are more deliberate than your brook trout. You have to wait until they take the fly and go down. We say to ourselves: 'God Save the Queen!' and then strike. Now let me show you. You're using the right fly."

And show me he did. He pulled up his boots and he got me down on my knees and since my Wellingtons were short and the banks very wet I was soon soaked (yes, three days of stiff rheumatism were worth the cost). From his kneeling position he took the line off the water with a steeple cast, then snaked it out straight as a rule above a feeding fish; the fly drifted slowly, was sucked under and — "God — Save — the — Queen!" — he cocked his wrist and the trout was on. Together we took a pair, his, the first, going over 2 pounds. I have always thought that the striking of a fish was the most delicately timed act in angling. Now I was watching a master working with a rhythm and restraint I had still to acquire.

Sometime towards three o'clock the river quieted down and I retired to my hut to a chicken sandwich washed down with tea and an apple — but with the door open so that I should know as soon as a new hatch reanimated the stream. Boots off, toes flexing, I wondered what to use in the afternoon light — Lunn's Particular? Greenwell's Glory? Certainly a Houghton Ruby on the pool below the bridge.

But my feeling when the fish began feeding again at five was of abundance and futility. All about me was an abundance of strong and challenging trout and such was their cunning there was little I could do to lure them. At the top of the island was a rowboat moored to the bank and close to the gunwale a fish was making large rings, but I despaired of reaching him from below for the wind either blew my fly into the cockpit of the boat or too far to the left. "In my country," I explained to Mr. Mott, who had rejoined me, "I should go above him and drift the fly down."

"Oh, that wouldn't do, sir; Miss Potts wouldn't like it," he commented. "The Test is for upstream dry fly only."

I had my reprieve at dusk when the cuckoo was calling, and when I took another 2-pounder on the Ruby at the tail of the pool. Lightheaded and pleased with myself — I had been on the water nine hours — I left the fish lying in the net after having put the priest to him, and wandered along the bank, false casting to dry my fly. There was a small commotion in the carrier to my right; I tiptoed up and let the fly drop; there was an explosion and from the feel I was into something bigger, with my net hopelessly beyond reach. We played each other up and down the narrow stream until my neighbor from the beat below chanced by on his way home and rescued me. "But you really should carry your net," he admonished as he weighed my prize, "otherwise you may find it rather awkward."

The two brace that day were beginner's luck and on my return visits I have never done better. Back home in Boston I told all this to Ferris Greenslet, whose fishing expeditions were coming to an end, adding for his editorial approval that when my two days were over I drove on to Oxford, presenting one brace of trout to John Masefield at Abingdon and the other to Sir Isaiah Berlin. That Christmas Ferris gave me a copy of the English classic *A Summer on the Test* by John Waller Hills and this wise and leisurely book with its lovely plates by Norman Wilkinson deepened my appreciation of a river where the artificial fly was fished upstream by men who might have seen and talked to Shakespeare, and where in early times lines made especially for fly fishing were tapered down to a single horsehair. "How," Mr. Hills writes, "would you like to kill a four-pounder on a single horsehair with no reel?"

On subsequent visits it pleased me to think that I was on a stream men had loved and struggled with for centuries, where Sir Humphry Davy cast his fly, where Landseer and Turner fished and then sketched for the Houghton Club journal their favorite pools, where Palmerston, Lord Grey, Andrew Lang and even perhaps Izaak Walton may have felt a little of the futility that was mine. Thus far my longest stay at Leckford has been two days and a half and always in early spring but a man may dream and mine is to have a week on the Test when the mayflies are hatching.

In my exuberance on the Test I am often treading my beat before the first hatch of flies has brought any fish to the surface and it took many defeats before I learned that the wise trout will be frightened down by any one of several warnings in the brightness of noon: by the flash of the rod or by the angler's shadow close to the bank, or by awkward casting which produces a drag in the line or sends the leader like a gleaming arrow across the fish's window. The magic hour comes with the dusk when there may be such an abundance of flies that the water almost seems to boil with the avidity of the feeding fish. The old and crafty angler will

take advantage of this. I observed a retired colonel, rather gimpy in the leg, who conserved his strength for the fading light. He made his first appearance after tea when with his landing net as a cane he would pace his beat, not softly but stamping his heels at the water's edge. This had the effect of driving out the fish that had been loitering under the bank; he would mark the location of the larger and return to the lodge for his early supper and when he reappeared with his rod and evening flies of a large enough pattern for him to see he netted as fine trout in ninety minutes of this gloaming as we who had been at it all day.

I was never introduced to this character who lived to himself and his memories as some anglers prefer to do. The habitués at Leckford who went out of their way to befriend me were Miss Charyl-Hinton of the peaches-and-cream complexion and Captain Dunlop, a hearty veteran of the First World War. She was the most graceful dry-fly caster of her sex I have ever watched, she had fished the Test since childhood as a companion to her father, himself an expert, and proposals of which she must have had dozens did not lure her from the river. The largest trout in our fridge were invariably those she had netted. Captain Dunlop was an exemplar of English hospitality: if I had no car, which was usually the case, he would drive me to my beat before he went off to his own and would of course pick me up when dark fell; he made up the deficits in my fly box with flies he had tied himself and he gave me invaluable tips. "You'll be fishing Beat 11" he would remark. "Lovely water, lovely water and the swans won't bother you. The bigger fish come from the reeds directly across from the hut and they won't show till the evening. Then put on a Houghton Ruby and don't fret, my dear boy, if it sinks a little. They sometimes like it that way."

Beat 11 is at some distance across the valley from the lodge and it offers the widest variety: very fast water holding some stout rainbows, a long stretch through the water meadows that must be fished from far back and the wide swan's bay opposite the hut which I purposely saved till the last. It fell out as the Captain predicted: in deepening dusk I put on a Houghton Ruby and when, to be honest, it had become a little waterlogged I felt the strong down pull of a heavy fish, and set the hook. I couldn't move him. With my rod bent double I got below him, to add the current to my persuasion, but he had gone to grass and his hold on it and his weight made him immovable, though I could feel his bulling. I thumped the butt of the rod against my palm, which sometimes gives shivers to a sullen fish, but not to this one. And then came the Captain's horn tooting for me to join him on the road at the top of the ridge. I didn't want to call; fish are sensitive to sound and it might make this one strain the harder. Again a long note from the horn. "Coming!" I shouted, involuntarily. "Coming." It would be such a triumph for both of us if I could bring this big boy to the net. But I mustn't keep the Captain waiting; slowly I forced the bowed rod above my shoulders. Would he come up? Would the fly hold? . . . No. The sudden slackness told the story and I reeled in.

My visits to Leckford, never for more than forty-eight hours, always presented me with something memorable: now it would be the high bank above the drive with masses of cream and yellow daffodils, now at dusk the elastic colloquy of whippoorwills across the valley; once on a warm bright day when I had fished too long in rubber pants I was seized with cramps in both legs and lay writhing on the meadow till they passed, and again, the moment when knowing I could not be in England when the mayflies came I decided to experiment with one prematurely — and was happily surprised when a good trout came up for it greedily and was hooked. I even encouraged my English authors to work with me at the lodge on their manuscripts, and on my desk in Boston is a photograph in color of my favorite beat sent me for Christmas by Joan Bright Astley. How it invites the mind.

One Sunday evening as I was on my way back to Andover and the City I asked the driver about the upper reaches we were then passing — was the fishing here as good as at Stockbridge. "Oh, no, sir, the stream hereabouts is filthy and polluted." "The Test?" I said, incredulously. "Yes, sir." By such a narrow margin does even the greatest river survive.

Much of the best fishing in Britain is in private hands and the pleasure of staying in a well-served country house and visiting the family pools at will has been repeatedly conferred upon me by two Conservative Members of Parliament, long good friends of each other who came to be good friends of mine. Sir Frederic Bennett, the younger of the two, has his favorite domains at opposite ends of the Islands which suits his temperament as he loves to be in motion: his

9-gun castle at Kingswear, built in the fourteenth century
to command the entrance to the River Dart, is his seat in
his constituency, which embraces Torquay and Dartmouth,
whereas his country estate Cwm which he hungers for in
Recess is far to the north, high in the Welsh hills. Freddy
has the powerful legs and torso of a sprinter which he was
in school; he is one of the best shots of his generation and
with his gun and his beloved Labrador, Twist, he could
spend all day on the Welsh moors and never tire. He is an
impulsive, warm-hearted collector, of guns, dogs, houses,
rare birds, and of motors each one faster than the last — but
not of fish. The little lake at Cwm which he assures me he
stocks for my benefit (and that of his nephew David) is apt
to be glacial and windswept when I am there in April and
like most non-anglers Freddy soon grows impatient;
whether he is rowing me or accompanying me to the water
of a friend his attitude becomes that of a mother forcibly
feeding Junior some spinach: the trout are there and it is
plainly willful of me not to heave them in without all this
dither, fly-changing and delay. The fish know this: "Old
Fred is above," they say. "Let's skulk and annoy him," and
they send a boy to do a man's job.

There may be a good hatch of flies at Cwm in the heat of
July but I am never there to see. When I push out on that
rhododendron-bordered pond the trees are not yet in leaf
and the surface, slightly warmer than ice, is disturbed only
by the wind from the Arctic. In the distant past Fred's
father, a member of Lloyd George's Cabinet, stocked Cwm
with brown trout and rainbow which, it is assumed, have
grown to great size. Pointing out the spot where little
David last summer "caught a really good trout on a worm,"
Fred shoves me away in the canoe and with irrepressible
energy goes forth to feed the peacocks, Canada geese, and

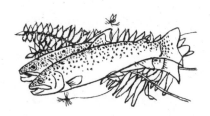

jungle fowl, to build a fox-proof pen for the Muscovy ducklings or to discuss with his farmer the possibility of liberating on the wildest down his small herd of Bagot goats.

It is my private suspicion that in this 40° water with so little feed of any kind, the fish shrivel, but I go about my business, casting a March Brown into the shallows where the vinegar sunlight may have attracted a little life, knowing full well that two hours later I shall be summoned with "God's teeth, nothing but that tiddley? What *have* you been doing! Well, come on up and have some tea with my mother." And seated on the floor, boots off, reaching now for the warmth of the coal fire, now for the plum cake, I shall have this solace from Lady Bennett: "Freddy's father couldn't catch them either; it used to make him *so* annoyed!"

(Actually — a word the English employed with special emphasis — the trout did shrink. After years unnumbered a sudden violent hurricane burst the dam at the outlet and the nine million gallons of water and its contents surged down the valley, into the river Angle, and thence into the tumultuous Dovey. Within the fortnight the natives were capturing strange fish with monstrous heads, which an expert identified as rainbows, whose skulls but not whose bodies had grown during the decades, gaunt souvenirs of the elder Sir Frederic's planting.)

I was saved from total defeat by Freddie's neighbor Ralph Beaumont, who had converted two tarns for his own amusement: into the small blue bowls of mountain water on the very crest of the tawny downs he had introduced grass and brown trout; there was not a tree or bush to grant protection and here on one noon picnic, under leaden clouds and a northeaster that cut to the bone, we had to form the traditional British square to preserve any warmth in the women and children in the center. But on clear eves when the wind had dropped Rafe and I had good sport, using a black Zulu, and returned with enough for a full platter. For Freddy, loving his heritage as he does, it is a grievance that I come so early, two months before the sea trout begin to fill the pools of the Dart and the Dovey. By late June, he swears, Edwards, his eighty-year-old gillie, and I could catch them with our hats; yes, but by then the Atlantic salmon are coming upstream in Eastern Canada, and that is the closer call.

But as I have already told, it is quite a different story in Hampshire where my other cordial host, Sir Hugh M. Lucas-Tooth, has his unique estate, on the Avon, one of that noble trio of rivers, the Test, the Ichon, and the Avon, all of which empty into the Southampton estuary. In 1945, looking for a place not too far from London — two and a half hours, by road — where Laeta, his wife, could garden and he could fish or shoot on weekends, they found their heart's desire at Fordingbridge. I call it a water house for it stands as close to the river as the banks allow and the sound of water rushing through the weir is music to my ears. The foundations of the house are very old and the weirs themselves are weathered and immemorial. There may have been a dwelling here in Roman times; the Romans were fond of fish and oysters, indeed it was the discovery of a mass of oyster shells plowed up by a nearby farmer that led to the excavation of a large-scale Roman villa.

Sir Hugh can never tell when the salmon will arrive: he has killed a 34-pounder on March 4, yet a year later no fish appeared until early May when he killed two each day he fished until the run was through. The run is a short one, some fish lingering on to spawn in his waters, most after a day or so moving on to the redds upstream. The take on his five pools, which are twenty miles in from the sea, varies with the height of the water and those I have hooked in the early spring hang in the Upper Weir Pool, at the point of suction where the water surges through, or down and around the corner in Willow Run where they lie close to the undercut bank or right across the stream where a large fly so eagerly clings to the brambles on the bank. In a good year Hugh and his guests will account for forty fish; a more moderate run yields twenty-five, and he apologizes for the fact that my largest was only 23 pounds.

Lady Laeta has a green thumb and her flower beds flourish, daffodils and grape hyacinth, bordering the paths to the water's edge. It is not uncommon to watch from her guest bedroom a salmon indolently disporting in the slack water of her rock garden.

Hugh is an erect and sandy Scot; he tops me by four inches and it is always a surprise, considering his breadth of shoulder, to find that his extra pair of fishing trousers have a tighter waist than mine. Whether he is fishing a Golden Sprat with his greenheart rod or casting a fly with his 14-footer of cane, from the first cast to the final gaffing he is an angler alone. He will tolerate no gillie here and watching him dominate his fish is a picture and a lesson in competence. "You must dominate your fish!" he calls to me as I come scrambling after mine and remembering how he does I try to imitate.

When the salmon are gone and the river is down he wades

upstream dry-flying for the brown trout; his log shows an average of just under 3 pounds with a few going above 6. In June with his cousins he fishes the prime salmon rivers in Scotland, including the Dee and the Spey; grouse shooting calls him in August and when Parliament convenes in the autumn he goes down to Fordingbridge for the weekends for the ducks that will be flying till January. Not a bad calendar.

There are times, especially in his lowest pool at the tip of the woods, where the wading is sticky, when Hugh has his hands full. Laeta, a Scot herself, tells it with her mischievous smile. "Hugh was very late so I went to find him and there he was down by the trees, mucking about, saying that he'd had the beastly fish on for almost an hour and he didn't know how much more of this he could take. 'I have my garden shears,' I said. 'Shall I cut the line?' That seemed to fetch them both."

9. *CLOSER TO HOME*

OPEN country where one can be alone is still to be reached within sixty-five minutes' drive from the Boston State House. My desire for a hideaway close to town where I might find trout and good company on a May evening or solitariness in the early spring and late fall was gratified when I was elected a member of the Tihonet Club.

Tihonet is the name of an old and minute community inland from the sea on Cape Cod where the cranberry bogs and scrub pine begin, a slightly undulating plain of sandy soil and ponds stretching mile upon mile. In the past the community depended not on berries but on bog iron, chunks of which still lie on the surface. Slug Brook, which I wade occasionally, with its bottom as red as rust, got its name from having supplied slugs for the Revolution. Our clubhouse was originally a boardinghouse for the management of the ironworks, whose produce was floated on barges down a narrow canal and then loaded aboard the schooners in the harbor. When all this was put out of business by Mesabi, the land was taken over by A. D. Makepeace, who developed the bogs into a cranberry empire which today produces nearly a tenth of America's crop. The bogs, the largest of which stretch for half a mile, are divided by dikes, irrigated by springfed brooks that run cold through the hottest summer, and are covered, when frost threatens, by water from reservoirs which are banked up at the head of each big bog. There are native trout in the brooks, and the browns, squaretails and rainbows, when introduced in the reservoirs have grown to good poundage.

In 1893 a group of Boston anglers, led by Frank Benson, the artist, asked Mr. Makepeace for permission to fish for the native trout in the bog brooks, provided they did not set foot on the cranberry plants (since the streams are seldom as wide as ten feet, this means wading, or the bowman casting from diminutive canoes). A gentleman's agreement was entered into which still survives, the proprietor approved of our stocking a number of reservoirs and generously endowed us with a clubhouse. At first the membership was limited to fifteen, then as it moved up to the present limit of thirty (and wives) the native spawned trout did not suffice and, like other clubs, we adopted the put-and-take policy of planting some 1700 fish each year. Only in the reservoirs and wilder pools do they carry over and grow.

I shall tell of the fishing in a moment but first a word about the house to which, over the years, the members have added distinctive touches. To the right of the stairs as you enter is the Mud Room with bootjacks for those grown portly, scales to weigh the fish, and an icebox to keep them overnight, racks for those who carry the canoes on the top of their cars, on the mantel a photograph of President Calvin Coolidge in a starched collar looking quite cross as he steps out of a canoe; opposite the mantel, a poem illuminated with the more illustrious flies and on the walls tracings of the record trout — rainbow, squaretail, or brown — drawn on shingles, on brown paper, or slate, with the weight and the captor's name. In the corner is a large stand of oars and paddles.

Fish weighed, boots off, and hands clean, you move into the living room for the anticipated warmth and cheer. This is heated by a Franklin stove on cold nights and what one remembers are: the Morris chairs which through long sitting provide the perfect cavity for tired backs, photographs from Tahiti of ladies in undress, Benson's map of all our water with the spots indicated where he took his biggest (one suspects, with worms), two shelves of books, some by members, all of trout and salmon, a backgammon table

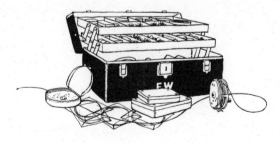

with dusty pieces in place which haven't been used since the 1920's, Bob Bellow's watercolor of this very room as it was fifty years ago with the fire blazing and the walls then tinted crimson, a logbook to record the day's catch, and hanging on the wall above it an ancient photograph of the bog iron works and that famous French lithograph *Un Rêve,* which reveals to the naked eye what the little woman is up to while her man is on the stream.

The dining room to the rear is capacious enough for twelve at table. It, too, is heated by a Franklin stove and the senior member present is privileged to sit with his back to it; the watercolors are by members, including Benson; the sideboard gleams with shakers and glasses of every depth; and in one corner Bob Bellows left his line drying on the wooden spindle the last time he fished, and there it remained for eighteen years. We are served by our loyal housekeeper who cooks hot suppers for us on spring nights when every other housewife on the Cape would damn us for being so late.

Until recently the house was lamplit and the plumbing outdoors. When James Parker donated the funds to install a proper john upstairs it became known as the Parker Memorial and the sign above it, in the secretary's script, reads, "Please use this contraption exclusively and eschew the front porch. The neighbors have complained." The handiness of this gadget was even better appreciated when the wives joined us. The feminine bar was first lifted with the understanding that they could spend the night only when it was sure no male members wanted to use the Club. Now couples come down together to make a foursome and the exclusive "For Men Only" atmosphere is pervaded by the hint of Chanel No. 5.

As one moves on in angling it is natural to associate certain streams with certain men. Tihonet to me will always mean Dick Danielson, my partner. It was he who engineered my election and it was with him that I first fished here in summer days when we had the club to ourselves. Dick, a six-footer, handsome, and one of the truly gallant men I have known, was a tackle at Penn Charter and as a freshman at Yale, and the M.F.H. of the Groton Hunt for most of the years he edited the *Sportsman*. But his superb physique was worn thin by illness, and after an incredible operation which gave him ten years to live, he still fished at Tihonet when it was a miracle that he could fish at all. He used to say that he was rationed to 85 pills a day; yet even after both his hips had been broken he managed somehow to scrabble down the bank and endure for an hour the bow seat in the small aluminum canoe before the pain drove him ashore. It was his last touch with the out-of-doors and he loved it.

The picture I hold is of Dick in the lamplight, in one of the Morris chairs, glass in hand, reliving his youth in those stories which gained in every retelling, of his first year in the class of Chauncey Brewster Tinker, his favorite teacher at Yale; of his rivalry and friendship with that redheaded classmate Sinclair Lewis, of his test in Chicago when he jumped from teaching schoolboys to investment banking, of the night at the Tavern Club when coming in late he had almost assaulted Waddy Longfellow with a beer bottle, mistaking for a burglar the little figure crouched at the round table, sleeping it off after the lights had been extinguished; back to Dakar and to the Inauguration in Liberia which he attended as Military Attaché to Admiral Glassford, when the flags of the United Nations, which fluttered above the reviewing stand and which had been hand-colored by the schoolchildren, suddenly released their tints in a cloudburst, and Dick in his dress uniform found himself inundated with vermilion; back to Marseilles in 1918 when as a young captain in Intelligence, he had requested and been refused permission to cross the Spanish border and kill the German agent who was directing the submarine tracking of our transports. "I knew where he was to be found, and I'd have killed him," Dick said simply, and I believe he would.

One morning at Tihonet I had driven the car to the upper reach of A.D.M. bog and was unstrapping the boat from the rack while Dick with his rod and crutch went limping down to the brook. I thought I heard a thud and when I turned he was on his knees propped up with his left hand, while with his right, tip up, he was playing a heavy fish. I came running. "Not a bad fish," he said, looking up with that beatific smile. "I wish you'd been here to see him take it."

The original members in the days before the automobile would pair off and be trundled out in a buckboard to their chosen stream where they would be deposited with their canoe and sandwiches for the day. Now, with cars and more water available, we decide at breakfast where we shall go and if the first try proves unresponsive we mosey about looking for something better. There are four bog brooks which take the better part of a morning to fish thoroughly: Wankinko, the narrowest with undercut banks and holes

too deep for wading, but the very devil to fish when the wind is from the west; A.D.M., the coldest and a fine spawning ground until the advent of DDT with which the bogs are sometimes sprayed; Frog Foot, known as "the fish market" because of its abundance, and totally unprotected from sun and wind, and Maple Springs, which has the finest blueberries as well as four of the best pools. There are four large reservoirs, two the size of small lakes, a President's Pool at the foot of one spillway, so named because the president of that era had difficulty taking trout anywhere else and so it was reserved for him. Wildest of all is the Upper Reservoir Stream, a thread of deep water winding under trees and between dense bushes whose branches catch everything but a roll-cast, that hoop-like cast that wheels the fly forward. Small wonder that some sporting characters survive; in the late fall, I like to paddle up here not to fish but to scout, and I am always surprised to find such hefty fish who dart ahead of me under the canoe to their refuge in the roots.

The wind is our chief adversary on the Cape and one afternoon in late April, having fought it profanely in open water with no result, young Ted and I paddled into the thickets of the Upper Reservoir stream as our only chance for protection. He was in the bow, I in the stern, and impatient: the wind had exasperated our teamwork and I was already beginning to think of bourbon on the rocks. Fortunately the water was high and the ridge to the west shut off the gusts. Ted is a very deliberate fisher, and never more so than this late afternoon so it seemed to me; for this dark water he prefers a silver-bodied streamer with jungle cock head and I must say he was retrieving it deftly. The sun had set by the time we approached the T Pool, the water turning to jet in the fading light; here the stream takes a left angle and the brook flowing in at the crossing of the T makes this an exceptionally broad and lively bay surrounded by alders. The thought of bourbon and supper hastened my paddle. "Well, that's about it," I said, as he netted his third small fish. "It'll be dark before we get back to the car." But he was still intent. "There's that deep water to the left," he said. "We'll never hit it under better conditions. Darndest Last!" So the canoe crept on, past the dying oak whose roots are half exposed, with the fly flicking the dark stream.

Suddenly a hump of water moved toward us; there was a surface disturbance, the tip of the rod went down and the hook was set. It was a big fish as we could tell from one glimpse and it fought in swift slashing runs, not leaping like a rainbow. I back-paddled for the deep water but the trout, anticipating me, had already crossed under the canoe in his rush downstream — and would the leader give? We followed him down through the pool and into the next, taking great care to dislodge him from his grassholds along the bank. Twice the man with the net, myself, failed to intercept and then at 8:25 the great beauty, his strength spent, came dripping aboard. After a struggle like that the thought of releasing the fighter stays the hand, the priest is always reluctant. Two pounds, ten ounces, he weighed, something of a record, and an evening etching we both treasure.

One comes to Tihonet for many reasons: to rusticate in this unmarred Cape country; to surprise into flight the osprey, the mallard, the partridge, and the great blue heron who with his razor-sharp beak takes far more trout than we do; to make our peace with the nesting redwing blackbird and to be scolded by the kingfisher. Here I have watched a huge mother turtle as she dug her nest in the hot sandy road at the top of our dike, and been startled by the snort of a deer ten feet from my shoulder as I stood fishing the Frog Foot. One comes here for the challenge of placing a dry fly in a four-foot stream between undercut deep banks, with the wind always in one's face, and for the black stillness of the water in the reservoirs after sunset; one comes for the vast openness of bog and brook and dike unhampered by fence or house, for the color of the bogs, ever changing from rusty red to green to burgundy, for the soft air and high clouds, and always for the fishing and the friends.

10. *RETURN TO THE NORTHWEST*

IN fishing as in love there is the innocence and surprise of
the first rapture and the joy, more deeply felt, of renewal. On two short visits as Jim White's guest I had lost
my heart to the Northwest Miramichi, that wild, narrow
stream in the Fraser Forest, but it was not until July
1951, when young Ted was sixteen and I was feeling flush,

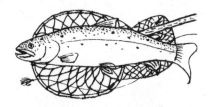

that I was seized by the desire to take the family up there for a week. I asked Jim if there was any opening in the Club schedule, and when word came back that we could have Camp Adams from July 14 to the 23rd, we invited my brother-in-law, Frederick Watriss, and his wife, Mary Elizabeth, to join us. It was short notice and family complications tied her down, but Fred was eager to come.

At luncheon the week before our departure Jim (who was lending the Weekses the rods and reels we needed) fired up our imagination. "The salmon will have moved to the upper pools when you arrive," he said. "That's why they're sending you to Adams. The woods and the river can warm up very fast, so pray for a good rain to freshen the pools. Be sure you have enough line-dressing and don't hesitate to use the dry fly. If the water is really low, your best chance will be in the early morning and after sunset."

"What about Dam Camp?" I asked for my memories centered in that lower camp with its noisy falls.

"It'll be open," Jim replied. "You might fish your way down and spend the night — that way you'd get to see the whole five miles of Club water. I doubt if there'll be anything but grilse in the lower pools. The mature fish will be up at Adams — or beyond."

In Anne Morrow Lindbergh's famous book *North to the Orient,* telling of the adventurous flights which she and Charles made to the Far East in their two-seater, there is an early passage in which she struggles to keep her indispensables within the weight limit Charles had set. Weight is no problem when you're traveling in a beach wagon but remembrance is, and Fritzy, young Ted and I each kept lists of what not to forget. Mine read:

> Gin and Bourbon
> Lollacapop
> Salted Nuts
> Extra Shoelaces
> Waders
> Flashlight
> Petit-beurres

(Lollacapop is an insect repellant with a tar base and such a reek that it keeps all human life at a distance; Petit-beurres are our favorite biscuit for between-meals.) Ted's list was of nothing but flies. Jim's fly boxes spread out a rich assortment but they were our reserve; it was time we began our own collection and Ted wrote out an order that would have staggered an Indian rajah. "Listen, brother," I cautioned, "those Hardy flies cost a dollar apiece!" This did not faze him; his eye was tempted by Jim's gaudier patterns. "What's that one, Pa?" "A Durham Ranger," I said, "good in high water." Six Durham Rangers, he wrote down. "And this?" "A Lady Amherst," I said, "too pretty to be useful." "How do you spell Amherst?"

Fred's beach wagon was loaded to the roof when we took off for Fredericton. Freddie is my wife's half brother; we had kept an eye on him during his schooling in New Hampshire and when he came down to pull an oar and take his degree at the Massachusetts Institute of Technology, he occupied a special place in our affections. Now he was in his mid-thirties, tall, quite sure of himself, and like all engineers, able to do almost anything with his hands. Indeed, on a trip to the far north which he made with Jim Rowlands to photograph the breeding grounds of the Canada Goose, when the propeller of their guide's outboard dropped off in the middle of Hannah's Bay, with a squall coming, Freddie retrieved it and locked it tight with a nut he devised from a piece of old plumbing found in the bottom of the Indian's canoe. But of salmon fishing he knew as little as any of us.

Are the Weekses the only family to make false starts? We were ten miles gone when I suddenly remembered that I'd left my fish box, with all our flies, sitting on the dining room table. I could see just where it was and since there was no trace of it in the car we turned back. It was exactly where I said but this cost me some criticism which did not subside until, box secured and journey resumed, we entered the Maine Turnpike, at which point the overcast broke into a steady drizzle.

On a long drive to the north woods — ours was to be 560 miles — one begins in forethought that gradual identification with the river which will continue till the last day. Our rain-streaked windshield reminded us of Jim's prediction, and we hoped the storm would reach our river. If the rain lasts all night, I said, the river might go up two feet and in high, dark water like that we'd have to use wet flies, and big ones. As the only one who had been on the stream before I may have been tempted to speak like an authority for it was on this trip that Fred casually referred to me as "Father," a sometimes derisive nickname that has stuck ever since.

The rain never ceased drumming on the roof that first night which we spent in damp cabins north of Machias, and it was still falling the following afternoon when we came down out of the hills to the bank of the St. John River. What the first view of this broad majestic stream, of the tiny white churches with their tin roofs, of the vast water meadows and the spidery ferry does to me it must have done to thousands of other anglers in their day: it puts me in mind of the uncomputered millions of salmon that have swum in here since the dawn of time, and I feel I have taken my first step into an older, more primitive world. The illusion deepened at Alex Bell's where the good doctor answered the questions which I was guessing at on the drive up.

Camp Adams, Alex told us, was roughly sixty-five miles from the river mouth, the last stretch of private water before the spawning grounds or redds. The Northwest had one of the earliest runs of any river in eastern Canada, this may have been nature's answer to the fact that the fish were shut off from the upper river by a vast rock-ledge once the water dropped in midsummer. ("Can't it be blasted?" the engineer wanted to know.) To reach the spawning beds in safety the salmon had to evade the trawlers in Miramichi Bay, thread their way through thirty-five miles of commercial setnets, and then escape the angler. Yes, the commercial fishermen took ten fish for every one killed by a rod and it was well to remember that if a river was to propagate enough eggs to maintain its run at least one-third of the entering salmon must reach the redds.

The Northwest had taken care of itself up until the last five years when fry from a hatchery were introduced. The adult salmon spawn in the autumn, burying the eggs in the gravelly beds in the protected upper reaches. The fry — the under-yearling — emerges in the spring and grows to be a parr — you'll find them all over the place, as long as your middle finger and always ready to hit your fly. After three years he's about ready to go to sea, and in his third or fourth spring, now known as a smolt, he makes it downriver. The smolt is six inches when he enters the sea and the mystery is how he grows: after one winter he may re-enter the river as a small salmon or grilse, weighing 3 to 4 pounds, and if he remains a second winter or a third he'll return as a mature salmon averaging about 9 pounds on the North-west.

("Don't they grow any bigger than that?" asked Ted. "I'm coming to that," said Alex.)

The spawning is all done by October and some of the salmon slip back to the sea before the ice forms. Those that are icebound spend the winter in the river and when they emerge in the spring they have lost half their weight and are gaunt, tubular, and so hungry they'll hit anything. They're known as kelts, or black salmon, and they shouldn't be fished for but they are. Only about ten per cent of the salmon on the spawning beds ever get back to the sea but from that ten per cent come the really big fish who on their final re-entry may weigh 25 pounds or a good deal more, depending on the stream.

That was our first lesson in the life span of the Atlantic salmon, and coming to us in Alex's high resonant voice with that twinkle of humor which graced so much of what he said, it was something we were to remember and piece out with what experience taught us.

We made our departure by twilight but not before Alex had given young Ted, as once he had given me, a couple of his favorite Green Highlanders, and to me a complimentary license in the name of "Edward Weeks and party" from the Commissioner of Lands and Mines, which was all "Father" needed to confirm his authority. To Fred, whom he'd taken to on sight, he gave the promise that he'd drive up to spend a night with us at Adams. Ted, who was then in the throes of calf love, had the last word. "Dr. Bell," he called, as we started the motor, "if there's any mail, please be sure to bring it."

When we signed in at the gatehouse of the forest the next morning, Frank warned us that they had just come through thirty hours of rain and that we had to take it slow. Not that you can do much else on a lumber road that is conveying 10-ton loads of spruce, fir, and hemlock. The road is founded on corduroy, pierced by innumerable brooks, with a top cover of clay and rocks of all size. It is full of potholes and in places so narrow that truck and car cannot pass, in which case the car backs up to a dry siding and idles while the truck, with its logs always seeming about to burst out of their chains, scrapes by with the driver in his cab grinning down at you. The shoulders of the road are soft and slope down to ditches filled with standing water or, occasionally, a cow moose and calf. In low gear one weaves back and forth between the potholes with respect for the rocks that look immovable. I remember Jim White glowering at one some distance ahead and deciding not to dodge it with his low-slung Chrysler. The rock never budged but the differential case was cracked and had to be doctored by a garage crew from the settlement. Normally one travels in a cloud of dust, taking perhaps an hour to reach the 16-milepost where our guides would be waiting but on this bright, newly washed morning we crept and slithered; the brimming ditches were an ever-present trap and where the brooks had burst through their culverts planks had been placed across the running water. It was my job to walk ahead and make sure that Freddie's front tires were aimed at the center of each plank, and then the rear end ditto. It was slow, edgy driving and luckily for us no truck appeared.

Always it is Henry Waye's sprightly figure we first see, waving us in toward the black tarpaulin Bear House in the clearing. The Bear House holds our reserve supplies and is so called because the bears raid it. Henry, who had broken me in, is a sandy Scot with merry eyes and he is our Greek messenger: to our opening question, as we shake hands all around, "Henry, how's the river?" he returns a reply laconic yet never without a trace of hope. On this occasion it was: "A great head of water. Dark and dirty now but when it clears it should bring the fish up."

With him were his tall sons, Harry and Blair, Harry, a former mechanic in the Canadian Air Force and Blair with his hazel eyes and high Scots coloring as fine-looking a young guide as one would hope to see. They made short work of transferring the contents of the beach wagon to the bed of Henry's wagon, duffle bags and liquor going in first, rods and light stuff on top and a tarpaulin lashed down to keep things from leaping out. (My Montague rod — now Ted's — did shake free and was found the next day lying in the grass between the deep ruts.) Clucking to Monarch and Queen, his farm team, as they take the hills, grinding away at his brake on the rocky slopes, Henry would make it to camp faster than we, the wagon lurching and heaving like a small boat in a rough sea.

We took it on foot for what Jim White described as "a good fat hour and a half's walk" — "fat" relating to what comes off you. Only on the ridges was the going less than mushy; the slopes were a running brook and the bottoms a quag. As we sweated through the bug dope the blackflies became more attentive but there were always distractions: we saw a chipmunk lose his balance, fall in and swim for his life; we surprised a cock partridge and a snowshoe rabbit with those big rear springs; we heard the wood thrush and the white-throated sparrow, and a long time after Ted had asked, "Aren't we halfway yet?" when we were plodding along in silence, became at last aware of that heavenly sound, the roar of the river, heard before we saw the blue through the thinning trees. We descended a long hill feeling lighter at every step, single-filed across the log bridge that spanned the brook flowing into Cook's Pool, and drew up beside the kitchen where we were greeted by Stanley, the cook, and Howard Copp, head guide and in his courtly, gentle way the king of our river life.

Our bags were on the porch of Adams, rods waiting to be mounted, the duffle stowed. The river describes a broad S at this spot, forming three pools with the camp itself in the inside center of the letter; from the porch looking upstream one can watch the angler working Corner Pool; directly down from the steps you are sitting on is Porch Pool, and around to the right, beginning at the horseshoe pitch and extending some distance below the kitchen and guides' cabin is Camp Pool, the deepest and widest of the three. There are wild strawberries and wildflowers in the pitch, and, when the fish are being salted, evening grosbeaks and purple finches. The air is filled with a running murmur more restful than the falls at Dam Camp.

Like all proper camps Adams is poised where one can see the river from every window. It has a screened porch, for reading and cocktails ("Keep that door closed!"), and an inventory of the high-stud interior would include a couch made of white birch, and chairs for weary backs, encircling the deep fieldstone fireplace, a chest of drawers with drink tray and bottles on top, an enlarged airmap of all the Club water, action photographs of fishermen and hunters, a moose head, handy for drying things, and a spindly little desk no one has ever been known to use. There is a rudimentary medicine cabinet, a shelf of old whodunits and curtained off in separate wings two double bedrooms whose mosquito nets, with some assist from the river, quiet snores.

The river was boiling high and just as discolored as Henry said, so in mounting the rods we put on our heaviest leaders and largest flies, I a Jock Scot #4 and Ted a Durham Ranger. Leaving the camp pools till after supper, the four of us and our guides took the uphill half-mile walk to the Top of the Falls. This, we were to learn, is the most acrobatic pool. The falls are ninety feet across with the pool at the crest widening into shallows at either side. Standing well back on a rocky ridge the angler has the clear sweep of the upper river — and a fine sight it is at sunset — but his attention is concentrated on the handy water immediately below him which deepens as it approaches the lip. Into this he makes short, quartering casts in the fast moving slick and if his fly is taken it will usually be at the very brink with the instant question of whether the salmon will make his fight above the falls or go over. If he goes over, so do you, leaping, scrambling down from terrace to terrace of the falls until, luck being with you as you reel in the slack, you find you are still fast to your fish in the wider, deeper reaches of the Basin. The odds are heavily against anyone at the Top of the Falls because there is only a split second in which to set the hook and an accurate bookkeeper would show that two out of every three fish that are hooked here fight free.

The Basin, at the foot of the falls, is a dream pool demanding longer casts and more deliberate skill. From the white water to the shallows at the outlet is a full seventy-five yards and the strong current is intercepted by thin rocky ledges on the longest of which, with a depression known as the Pulpit in its center, we do our casting. There are also huge boulders from the top of which one can try the choppy turbulent water closer to the falls although here as in all pools fed by falling water it is my observation that the closer one gets to the drop the less chance there is of attracting a fish. In the deep trough they seem intent only on their next upward leap, not on smacking a fly.

When inhabited, the Basin holds fish everywhere, some within fifteen feet of the Pulpit, most across the channel and up, and in clear water they are to be seen, the mature fish, fins and big tails waving, like underwater battleships, and beside or behind them, in threes or fives, their destroyer-escorts, the grilse.

Forty yards across are the rockfaces and pointed spruce of the opposite shore, a high rugged backdrop of which one is indistinctly aware; but one is acutely aware of the wet fly whose arc, like that of a minnow, one can clearly see, and when a fish rises to pursue it one's stomach quivers. Experience was to show that these two pools, Top of the Falls, and the Basin would yield more sport than any other spot; first we fished them together, then as I established the routine, we drew lots and paired off, alternating in the morning and after supper, letting the pools rest all afternoon. Just how many salmon the Basin is capable of holding I was not to discover until years later during the mining boom when a sassy young assayer, flouting every privilege, paddled his gleaming white canoe straight across the holding rocks at eleven in the morning and the scores of fish he dislodged in fright — there would be no fishing for them for several hours and little he cared — was a revelation of what a vast residential area this could be.

I drew first blood, killing a grilse in the Basin our opening afternoon, and like holding three aces in the first hand of a poker game it was to be my only triumph for some time. On our second day, more rain falling and wind strong from the west, it was Fred's turn to win and young Ted's to supply the comedy. Fred, from the Pulpit, hooked and netted a bright 9½-pounder, so fresh from the sea that the sea lice were still on him; the salmon came to a Cosseboom, a streamer fly, green and yellow with a squirrel tail, which showed up well in the murky water. It is funny when fishing under variable conditions how often the odd fly will prove to be the killer — and invariably it will be in short supply. We had no Cossebooms; Fred had two, and one of them was put out on loan to the Weekses, to be used sparingly and subject to immediate recall.

The Northwest is fished, as I've said before, from rocky stands or from log bugs, a two-log bridge, eighteen inches wide, reaching from the shore to a boulder on the edge of the channel. But the high water had washed most of the bugs downriver, obliging us to fish with our backs much closer to the spruce, and in the dilemma a backhand cast kept the fly out over the water and away from the branches more surely than if we retrieved the line, straight back over our right shoulder.

But a backhand cast with a line made heavy by the rain is not easy to handle and Ted had other ideas. In his big poncho, laced at the throat and stretching to his ankles, Ted turned his back to the river and proceeded to cast fiercely at the trees, paying out line until his fly came as close as he dared to the branches when with a half-pivot he would shoot the works over his shoulder toward the pool and let the current straighten things out. Fred, who was fishing with him, observed the technique in silence until the cocktail hour when with a passing reference to "an animated tent" he

went on to do a parody. This brought from Ted a series of retorts falling into a pattern: "That's a lot of bull — That's what you think — That's how it appears — but into the trees it shall go!" And into the trees it did go until the bugs were restored.

Not till our time was half gone did the river clear and begin to drop. Ted, fishing the Basin in late evening, hooked and played a strong salmon — and again he was dogged with laughter. Blair, who was guiding for him, put the long-handled net under the gleaming body, as it came coasting in now half-belly-up, but the fish still strong, burst the bottom right out of the webbing with his tail and went swimming back into the pool. Playing him through the iron mouth of the net, which Blair held shoulder-high, Ted steered the salmon back toward the shore where Harry was waiting with his net. And again the same thing happened — the fish again thrashed its way out of the bottom and swam free. Now he had to be played through two hoops and this took some doing as there were no more nets — or guides — available. Harry, who was closest to the water, saved the situation by wading into a slack stretch where with his iron rim he flopped the finally exhausted fish out of water. It was all done amidst shouts of mirth. Thirteen and one-half pounds he weighed on the Adams scale and only

Howard was not amused. All nets should have new bottoms before breakfast was his edict.

The long march downriver to Dam Camp we made on a bright cool morning with the wind from the southwest — "the wind the fish like best." The trail led us up a long ridge where roots gave a foothold and stubs to the toe, down into water meadows where wild iris and little pink orchids caught the eye; and always to our left the river fresh and sparkling with its sunpoints. We were in no hurry, touched every pool we passed, and Howard and I in the van had the kettle boiling for luncheon at the Ledges when the rear guard straggled in with big talk about the salmon Ted had hooked and lost in the Upper Glory Hole. All the men, it appeared, could hook a salmon except myself.

The Ledges in the full noon sunlight is an idyllic spot, a vast punchbowl with the swollen falls cascading down in foamy white and the granite walls topped by spruce and pine rising fifty feet above us, their green tips outlined against the blue sky. Down close to the water, trees rooted in the fissures cast a shade and the aeration of the falls gives such life to the pool that the grilse dance on their tails. Fish could be seen below us, entering the pool, leaping and splashing over the spillway at the lower end. Even after our three-hour walk food seemed superfluous at such a time and place. Fishing in turn, we all pricked grilse and Ted and I brought ours to the net. Then at last we were ready for mugs of tea, sardines and ham on big slabs of toast, and a stretch-out.

The last two miles to camp were hot going, the rocks and roots stubborn in their assault on wet and weary feet, and it was with such relief that we approached the white stockade of Dam and eased our shoulders free of the gear and fish-bag. George and Kathleen, Howard's son and daughter-in-law, promised to broil our grilse for supper and with that last spark of leadership I suggested it would be a fine thing to have a cold shower. I could rouse no enthusiasm from my languid followers but determined to set the example, anyway. In those days the bath at Dam was a narrow wooden hut with a tank overhead which the guide filled with buckets of river water, temperature 60° or something less. There was one window conveniently facing the Club porch and covered with cotton mosquito netting. In my bathrobe I descended, hung my towel and robe outside the door, entered, lost my balance on the soapy floor, grasped the chain which released the shower, and hanging from it, swung like a pendulum back and forth across the window, bellowing. The water was really piercing and my assertion later that it made the snow martinis taste better was received with the same derision as my performance on the trapeze.

Supper that evening was the first time any of us had ever tasted of Kathleen's cooking. There are certain advantages to the old-fashioned wood range and she knows them all. Her bread fresh from the oven, her ginger cookies and lemon meringue pie, her wild strawberry shortcake, her pancakes and her vanilla cookies with cream filling — these of course are adornments, but her staples, her homemade soups, the leg of spring lamb — one of Henry's — which she has been keeping on the snow for Sunday dinner, her salmon chowder and her broiled grilse qualify her as a Cordon Bleu of the Maritimes. She is redheaded with a clear white complexion, she loves the river and through her window she knows when fish are in Camp Pool and drops everything to come running when one is hooked, and the way she bosses big George and keeps her kitchen immaculate is a joy all around. She has something of Howard's turn of speech. On the hottest night when three of us sat studying the water in Camp Pool she suddenly roused herself. "Groan I may, but go I must," she remarked and went in to serve the supper from the torrid range.

At the table and on the trail next morning there was a covert exchange between Fred and young Ted about a "secret fish," evidently a salmon of some size they had seen in the Basin and hoped would still be there when we returned. When couples fish in rotation, each believes it has a special knowledge and a better way of doing things — this is what makes a horse race. Meantime there was the business in hand. We were on the trail before eight and in the damp and deeper shadows of the morning we woke, first Fred's Pool, then Dominick, and then the Ledges to life, Fritzy taking the largest of our eight grilse. We planned to lunch further upstream so as to give Ted another chance at the salmon he missed in Upper Glory, before the sun became too hot. Lunch for him was a bite and a promise and with Harry, his guide, he pushed ahead while the rest of us were letting our tea cool in the hot tin mugs.

Fritzy and I followed after, I with both rods and she with her camera around her neck. We were fifty yards from Upper Glory when we heard Ted shouting and she broke into a run. The river makes a deep turn here beneath a bluff and to reach the pool the angler climbs down a ladder and out along two logs to a flat rock inches above water. We arrived just as Ted, his rod as high as he could hold it, was leading the spent fish toward the rock where Harry crouched, taut and ready with the net. Fritzy, focusing at a glance, snapped the picture at the instant of surrender, as the net with the fish in it came out of water, and of the hundreds and hundreds she has taken since this is the prize.

We now had nine fish wrapped in wet burlap and

Howard announced that he would begin smoking them to-morrow. The trail home, which is mostly uphill, was lightened by our elation, and back in camp after hot shaves and in fresh clothes some of us were ready to tell the world. If I seemed silent it may have been because on this, the evening of the fifth day, I had yet to hook my first salmon and after supper by common consent I was posted to the Basin with one of Fred's deadly Cossebooms and with Fritzy, Howard, and Harry to cheer me on.

In the evening light the smooth dark water flowing past the Pulpit, where I began casting, is not easy for the eye to penetrate. Howard thought he saw a fish drift back in pursuit of the fly but there was no strike, and when, disconsolate, I turned the rod over to him, even the guide's expert probing, near and far, produced no result. We rested the pool and discussed changing the fly. "I'd leave it on," said Howard. "Should be a taker in this light."

Is it the irritation of repeated casts or the chemical prompting of light and time that makes a fish rise? After a pause I resumed my place with Howard crouched beside me. I made a twenty-foot cast which curved slightly toward the rockface, there was a streak of light under water, the tip of the rod went down and "There's your salmon," said Howard quietly. "Sure it isn't a grilse?" But the slow, heavy pull of the line was in itself an answer. "Shall I put some pressure on him?" Howard nodded and as the reel tightened and the leader came up, there on the surface, roiling, showing his big tail and black back, was a sizable fish. "There's your grilse," said Howard ironically. If the salmon went over the lower falls there would be little chance of holding him and for a moment he seemed headed that way. I jammed my thumb on the reel to keep it taut. Then the big boy turned and idled slowly down toward us into the clear quiet bay beside the Pulpit where all could get a good look at him; back he drifted into the deeper water, the fly evidently causing him no distress, and then once again started our way. "Howard, why not get the net under him if he comes all the way this time?" Howard already had the idea and the spoon had been submerged; the fish came slowly on, drawing ever closer to us until with a swift splashing heave Howard had him in the net and out of water. Only then did the salmon begin to fight and his thrashing nearly knocked the big man into the water. As he teetered on the rock edge Howard let out a roar and then plunged net, fish, and himself into the depression of the Pulpit while Harry came running to his aid with the flailing killer-stick. It happened faster than I can write it.

Measured and photographed under a flashbulb at camp it proved to be a cock fish weighing exactly 20 pounds, the largest to be killed in Club waters that year or ever since. "Damn you, Father," said Fred. "That's *my* secret fish and you've taken him with *my* fly!"

The "smoking" had begun before we were in circulation the next day and it is an art of which Howard is the master. The fish are cleaned, spread and salted on a drying table by the edge of the brook in back of camp. (The grosbeak are excited by the salt, so after dusk are the deer.) Close by the table so that Howard can watch the fire in its mouth is a wooden flue extending fifteen feet up the bank and into the base of a wooden hut, six feet square with a cap roof with open vents from which the pale blue smoke emerges. Here, after they are salted, the fish will be hung like pajama tops open to the smoke. Too often fish are hung so close to the fire that the smoke half-cooks and embitters the flesh. Howard is very particular about the length of the flue and the chunks of green oak and maple which must burn slowly

at its mouth; the smoke he fans is of just the right temperature to flavor but not dry up the natural juiciness of the
salmon, and his fish, which will keep for months, are such
a delicacy that we ask him to smoke all we catch until the
last two days of our stay.

Engineer Watriss had to satisfy himself about every
particular and indeed was helping to hang the larger fish
in the smokehouse when Alex Bell drove into camp in his
jeep — and for the rest of that day routine was forgotten.
The doctor brought messages and newspapers for the
guides, fresh provisions for the cook, beer for everyone's
lunch, and for Ted two letters. "Ted," he called, "I've got
something for you. They've been burning a hole in my
pocket." As well they might, being written with green ink
on pink stationery highly perfumed.

Gaiety traveled with Alex and permeated so much of
what he did. We urged him to set up his rod and then, leaving Ted to moon, we all went up to the Top of the Falls,
which we insisted he fish. He went at it fast and surely and
the moment a grilse showed as they do so vividly against
that clear bottom he whisked the fly back into the shallows
and nothing would serve but that Fred must take the rod.
When the fish hit and began to jump Alex was in his ele-
ment. "Don't let him go over, Freddie," he chortled. "Keep
him away from the falls!" But no light rod is capable of
braking a grilse in the first five minutes and when it did go
over, with Fred leaping down and scrambling in pursuit,
the doctor became Falstaff, exhorting, swearing, laughing
in his relish of every minute. Inclined to stoutness himself,
he loved to see others run.

At supper that night we told him our score: 7 salmon and
27 grilse with young Ted, who had killed four of the salmon,
top rod, and my 20-pounder, the largest. Alex pronounced

it a very creditable performance, better, he said than some of the members had done — thanks to the deluge before we arrived. If I accentuate the numbers it is because most innocents as we then were think of little else. How big and how many? It takes years of experience to cool down that obsession and some time more to reach the point where an angler would as soon release a good fish as kill it. This we were to learn by degrees in our identification with our river.

Slumber that night was punctured by the Doctor's snores which neither his sleeping bag nor the river could hush. But it was heartwarming to have him join with Howard and the others in our sendoff. Fred spoke for us all as he turned over the motor in the hot dust-streaked station wagon. "Mary Elizabeth just won't believe it," he said. "But it's going to be hard to have to wait for another fifty weeks."

So began a devotion which has never abated. The Club accommodated us when the members had had their fill and with each renewal we gained in our intimacy and knowledge of the river. The second year we went up in two cars setting a time when the caravan should meet at Vanceboro on the Canadian border, and with Fred and Mary Elizabeth driving from Concord and we from Beverly Farms we arrived within five minutes of each other. We made one small slip, however, for each of us brought along enough liquor for the party and as Canada allows the import of only one quart a person our surplus was too much to be winked at and had to be kept in bond at the Customs House. While Fred was attending to the red tape a young Customs officer, good-looking in his dark blue, drew me aside. "Sit down on this bench with me for a moment," he said. "I want to have a little straight talk about our rivers. You'll be going up to your club waters on the Nor'west and we all respect what you people have done to protect our streams in times past. But maybe it's been overdone. Some of your wealthy outfits only open their camps for three weeks or a month each year and they have wardens patrolling it when they're not there. We think this is wrong; we see no reason why those pools shouldn't be fished under regulation when the family or club has finished. I was brought up on a river; now I come home after five years in the army and I can't find any public water that isn't crowded to death. We shall have to do something about it."

He spoke with a genuine feeling I had to respect, and when that evening I related our conversation to Alex he nodded soberly. "That lad is more than half right," he said. "They do have a grievance and we shall be hearing more about it at Ottawa. There is a very definite movement to open up more and more public waters on all our big streams." Alex went on to say that the pools close to Adams and Dam had been bought from Crown lands by the Club at the close of the nineteenth century but that the pools in between and those at Stony Brook, the lowest of the camps, were leased to us and had to be bid for at auction every ten years. "The bidding is getting very rough," he said, "and it is the big lumber companies that are forcing the price up. They're building lodges where they can entertain the lords of the press, and they're greedy for more water."

The conditions to which we introduced Mary Elizabeth were very different from what they had been the year before. The temperature stood at 90° when we entered the breathless forest at eleven in the morning and each car was enveloped in a cloud of dust. Twice our little caravan was nearly blasted into the landscape by threatening lumber

trucks, traveling in their clouds of dust. The transshipment
of all our gear into Henry's wagon was a warm affair and
the trek into Dam where we were to begin our fishing
seemed endless. Mary Lib, comely, with an infectious laugh,
spent her girlhood in Atlanta, Georgia, where she acquired
among other things her love for gay clothes, her insatiable
curiosity, and the sense of order instilled into her two young
sons, Ricky and my godson Jimmie. She runs a trim ship.
But in Georgia one goes to the mountains when it gets to be
excessively hot, not into a baking forest. On that long walk
the black flies and mosquitoes followed us in swarms and
although she was coated with "Old Woodsman" she is al-
lergic to insect bites and could feel the swellings begin on
either temple and at the hairline. She did not say so at the
time, but as she trudged along in single file the thought
kept repeating itself, "It must be awfully good when we
get there to be worth all this!"

Dam Camp, which at high noon felt like Calcutta, began
to cool off when we had cocktails; we changed into heavier
shirts for the evening fishing and slept under blankets.
There were salmon and grilse in every pool, and in the hot
bright afternoons we could watch the family groups drop
back into the shade of a tree, or close to an inflowing cold
spring. Their disdain for any lure merited Howard's description — they were indeed "dilatory." We could spy
them from the high points, from the high rock at Caribou
and from the crow's nest above the Basin, and to Mary Lib,
to whom all this was new, the sight of those dark backs and
slowly waving fins and tails was an instant challenge. But
such fishing as we had came only in the early morning and
in the silvery dusk. Mary Lib lost the first salmon that she
hooked, not quickly but after a long fight, and through no
one's fault — the fly simply pulled out. In her tears and

tantrum she told off Fred and then Henry for not having done something about it while there was still time. As Henry put it — he wasn't sure if he would ever be forgiven. But she made up for all this a day later by bringing two good fish to the net.

In the hottest of all our summers our joy at Dam as night fell was in watching the salmon leap the falls. All afternoon they would circle round and round the big Camp Pool at the base of the falls where we could see them from above, impervious to any fly, intent only on the next stage in their journey upstream. Then in the semi-dark they would emerge like projectiles from the turbulent pool, aiming their leap at the very center of the falling water, a distance of eight feet, where the force must have been that of a fire-hose. If their aim was accurate they would hang there for a split second, quivering, before the propulsive tail and body drove them up the second half and we saw the big tail disappear into the smooth current at the very brink. But if they missed, the water would fling them to the rocks on either side with a report like that of a giant firecracker, and those side rocks of the waterfall were glazed and slippery from the accumulated scales. The trout would be the first to leap, then the grilse, then the mature fish, and seeing them at their acme was quite as good as seeing them smash a fly.

The zest for numbers was still clamorous in our blood the third year when thanks to our unseen benefactors, the Fred Smiths of Beverly Hills, each of the Weekses at last had his own rod, his own line to grease, his flies to protect. Luck determines whether your eight days will be foul or fair; this time we were greeted with the ideal: the river full and clear, the water temperature dropping during the cold nights as the thermometer went down under 40°, and the salmon, always a gentleman, not beginning to bestir himself until the sun had warmed the surface after breakfast. We started in the fast waters of Dam and followed the fish up to Adams and those calmer pools which are more susceptible to the dry fly. We ranged far and wide, taking fish from twenty of the twenty-three pools and by the final day the five of us had accounted for 22 salmon and 17 grilse, with young Ted again high rod — he had the bad grace to kill 4 salmon in one morning, which seemed disrespectful to his elders. Fritzy also did well, especially when little Billy, the cook's ten-year-old, was spotting for her; he had eyes like a gimlet and would dance with delight shouting, "Fritzy's got a salmon, Fritzy's got one!" when she profited by his directions.

Because the majority of our fish were mature we learned more about their strength and cunning than when the bulk of our catch were grilse. At Mountain Brook I had one brute on my line for a solid hour by the watch; I could not crank him up and although the guides tossed stones over him I could not move him. He anchored himself where brook and current met and the current was strongest and there he bulled, shaking his head and shaking it, until the aperture was large enough for the fly to be shaken free. At Camp Pool I became convinced that at the head of the pool where the spring flows in but down deep, was a veteran: she would

only come to my dry fly, which seemed to annoy her, after sunset; I saw her a couple of times and hooked her once but not for long. I think it was a big hen fish and that she was determined to stay right there and spawn when the spirit moved her. I made no change in her plans. And up in Basin Fred and I were both witness to Fritzy's struggle with a fish that might have broken all records: he wolfed her dry fly and went down, fought up current, rubbed line and leader against the outer ledge, and suddenly turned tail and bolted downstream, snagged the line against a half submerged log and when the guide waded out he was gone. An old Van Hoeff reel with its adjustable drag might have held him in the pool, though I doubt it, for a big fish in a swift and narrow river has all the odds if there is no boat for pursuit. In that rough terrain legs are not fast enough.

This summer for the first time I began studying the trail which is most readable after rain, when the pockets between the roots will have dried and the moist earth will tell who has passed this way earlier. One expects the print of deer and is always surprised by the larger evidence of moose: "Looks like somebody spilled a bag of prunes," remarks Henry, who is always notional. A lacerated dead birch shows where the bear has been grubbing for ants, and once I had the luck to intercept a doe between the path and the river's edge. Up she came, in steeplechase jumps, her white tail flying, so beautifully unerring as she spaced her springs between the boulders and the deadfall.

The mornings are the best, the trail then so fragrant and the green so moist. Head down, one takes in the little things. On either side of the path with its cover of spruce needles are masses of bunchberry, its square white blossom set off glossily by the six-pointed leaf. One looks for the white lady's-slipper, the clusters of lavender catnip, or the tiny pink colonies of twinflower; shinleaf, the forest lily of the valley, and in rare openings, lady's-tresses and the purple-fringed wild orchid. The trail to Stony Brook dips through some rich river soil where for twenty yards the growth is outlandish: masses of Queen Anne's lace standing shoulder-high ("stinkin' elders," Henry calls them), and topping them the fronds of the fiddlehead fern, from which we get a salad as delectable as cold asparagus. The logs which carry us across this mucky ground are guarded by a regiment of blue flags.

My feet are grateful for the moss which cushions the ledges. If it weren't for the thought of fish, I should study the mosses more closely, the plushy emerald green, the darker blue on the fallen logs, the needle moss like some tiny conifer. This green inlay is most vividly to be seen on the clearstone, the glistening white granite; here is a footstool for a Boston editor, if I could find a way of keeping the moss on it alive and the stone forever moist in my library!

It is two miles and a half from Camp Adams to Sam's Pool, and four pools to fish on the way. Walking that trail in waders in the early day, one feels like Mercury; the 10-foot rod is simply a longer finger; the musette swung from the shoulder, with its fly boxes and rain jacket, is no heavier than the bug dope on one's skin. Anticipation urges us, and if the heel skids on a slippery root it takes only an extra jump to restore one's balance. But it's a different story

four hours later when with wet and heavy feet we turn back
to camp. The arches have fallen, the toes cry out, the roots
and the stubbing granite become personally belligerent;
now a step wrenches the whole frame, and a mutter of protest ("Don't do that, you ape. Watch where you are going!
Damn it, not that way") breaks out. At such times I remember Elliot Farley, an angler who was hit by polio in
mid-life and crippled from the waist down. But with that
strength of arm and spirit which comes as compensation to
such sufferers, he would literally haul his way along the
trail, toiling half the morning to reach the pools. I think
how he must have studied every root, even the tiniest of the
moss flowers; temper subsides and I go in humbleness.

The average of one fish a day for each of us (not counting the three or four we rose and pricked and lost) is a
paltry total compared to what five rods might do on the
Restigouche or the Moisie; those larger, more bountiful
rivers which I know from brief experience, hold many more
and larger salmon. But for us it was good, nor could we
suspect that it would be our maximum, and that thereafter
the take on the Northwest would decline year after year
until it almost reached the vanishing point. The reasons for
this we could only guess at while we were on the stream but
the fatal truth is clear now. The fish and their fry were
being poisoned, first by the drenching of the stricken forest
by DDT in the fight to save the spruce from the budworm,
and second and more sinister by the lethal water pumped
out of the corridors of a zinc and copper mine and into a
feeder brook some fifteen miles below Dam Camp. It is
ironic that the pollution began just as biologists from St.
Andrews had established counting stations, traps below

and above the Club through which all migrants passed, in an endeavor to measure the growth and final destination of our salmon. Their purpose was not to scout for disaster but they ended by reading the temperature charts of a mortally stricken river.

It is not a pretty thing watching a river you love lose its life. Through this ordeal we took our bearings from Howard: he has been working on the Northwest for more than half a century; his devotion to it is inseparable from his devotion to his family and his comfortable farm back in the settlement. He tells me that the forest floor is now much clearer than it used to be; the slash and dense undergrowth are gone and through the aisles of trees one can see the spruce partridge. He tells me of how sweet a grilse can taste in their severe winter diet. I try to tell him what the woods and river give me: the feeling of privacy so rare in our urban life, the absence of litter and waste, the reassurance of unchanging natural beauty. Only by hints did we disclose to each other the dread that pollution had found its way to this wild place, and was killing it.

11. *FOREIGN WATERS*

IN the spring of 1959 our State Department invited me
to be one of a delegation of writers which was to be sent
to the Soviet Union that summer on a cultural exchange.
The other members were Arthur M. Schlesinger, Jr., the
historian, Alfred Kazin, the critic, and Paddy Chayevsky,
the playwright; we got along splendidly and as might be

expected we came to know each other rather better than the Russians by the end of the trip. It was a summer of glorious weather; Moscow was more receptive than usual because of the American Exhibition in Slovinsky Park which thousands patiently waited in line to see, day after day; and when shortly after our arrival it was announced that Khrushchev would visit the United States that autumn the curiosity which surrounded us was tinged with cordiality. The Moscow Writers Union looked out for us, put a car and driver at our disposal and the best quartet of translators I have ever worked with; they gave us spending money, arranged intimate picnics and supper parties with such distinguished members as Fedin, Simonov, Marshak and Ehrenburg, and they went further, they permitted Paddy to take colored movies and me to take with me my Thomas rod in its aluminum tube.

Carrying a fly rod in a tubular metal case over long stretches of the Soviet Union is a nuisance which would only be endured by an addict like myself, for it is a slippery object, given to sliding under one's seat in the plane and arousing suspicion in strangers who suddenly find it rolling underfoot. I had taken the rod with me on the chance that I might be invited to fish with Mikhail Sholokhov, who has a reputation for making big catches on the River Don. Or, failing this, I wondered if I might come within reach of one of the big pickerel that the Russians prize in their forest streams, But, up until our departure for Tashkent, I had not a single opportunity to take my rod out of its case. The lakes close to Moscow are well stocked with carp, which the Russians take with a crooked bamboo pole from which dangles a tiny baited hook and a glass bobber, the same equipment I had seen the Dutch using for the carp in their canals. I was out for a colder, more elusive prey, and my hopes had been dashed at Leningrad, where I was prepared to drive the eighty miles up the peninsula to fish for salmon in the Vuoski River, which had once belonged to Finland. But Mariam, our interpreter, said sadly that the authorities had told her the river was low, the water too warm, the fish not taking — a circumstance which I had already encountered, to my disappointment, in Ireland.

It was Konstantin Simonov who gave me a fresh spark, in the course of a delectable Sunday supper of pink vodka and smoked fish in his Moscow apartment. He was delighted to hear that we were going to Tashkent, and when the interpreter told him that I was an irrepressible angler, his face lit up. "Good," he said. "I shall write to my friend Hamid, and he will take you to the foothills of the Pamirs, where together you will catch the famous blue trout."

We flew the two thousand miles from Moscow to Tashkent in four hours and ten minutes, jet time, and when the delegation of Uzbek writers, led by bland, black-eyed Hamid, the secretary of their union, came down the ramp to meet us, I found that Simonov had been as good as his word. They nodded approvingly at my rod, and Hamid had driven to the airport in a sturdy new Land Rover, to show me what we would make the trip in.

"He says you will be leaving Sunday morning," the interpreter told me. "Perhaps as early as three A.M. Meantime they have fixed up a pretty crowded schedule for you."

Uzbekistan is one of the most Asiatic and pastoral of the sixteen Soviet republics. The Uzbeks are a sturdy, almond-eyed, swarthy folk, renowned for prodigious harvests of cotton, for the delicacy of their melons and grapes, and for their epic meals of pilaf and shashlik. Under their greatest hero, Tamerlane, they ruled the world for forty years. Then, in the sixteenth century, the belligerence went out of them and they reverted to a bucolic existence, which has only recently been disturbed. No Uzbeks, we were told, were used for fighting in World War II.

In the dry, baking heat of the following days, we were in constant transition between the twentieth century and the Middle Ages. Our hotel, modern but only half built, had French windows opening on to the plaza, with its splashing fountains and fine-looking opera house. The little flyspecked grill where we had lunch was half full of Uzbeks wearing their dark-blue skullcaps with silver embroidery, but beyond it through glass doors we could see the spacious high-ceilinged dining room with a dais for the orchestra. From the hotel we were driven to the market: the great trestles of Garden of Eden fruit and vegetables, presided over by striking Oriental types, some attracted by, some suspicious of Paddy Chayefsky's movie lens, were a picture which could hardly have changed since Tamerlane. On the slopes surrounding the market rose, layer upon layer, the ancient one-level houses of adobe. At the end of the market, where the cotton fabrics and scarves were displayed, squatted an old man beside a pile of hats of plaited yellow and green straw. "Fishermen's hats," said Hamid. "You had better have one." I found one to fit me for five rubles, and under the shade of its brim continued to suck the purple grapes, each half the size of my thumb.

The Uzbeks have the characteristic openhanded hospitality of pastoral people, and the welcome they gave us at the Writers Union was genuine. We talked to them about

their heritage. We questioned them about their history and archaeology and why they liked Hemingway ("Because he loves men"); it was apparent from what they said that they took naturally to folklore and poetry and that Hamid, their chairman, was the most successful of their native novelists. Our discussion was followed by vodka and supper, and then, under the stars, we were escorted to an open-air theater to see an Uzbek opera and ballet, the story a blend of folklore and Party line in which the handsome prince risks his own life in order to spare his slaves from execution. The costuming and acting were surprisingly good, and the singing of the women reminiscent of the Chinese.

Next morning, a visit to a cooperative farm. Well, I can take anything if there is a fishing trip at the end. We inspected the endless cotton fields and then, making a short cut, found ourselves suddenly in a grape arbor whose green and purple clusters were, some of them, the size of a man's head. We sampled our way along in the heat of midday and came to a rest house, a running brook, and, in the shade of a big willow, a table which was literally to groan with food. I thought each course was the main meal and acted accordingly. I sat to the right of the farm chairman, and he broke my bread for me, the crusty circular loaves, while we were being served the highly seasoned shashlik. I ate the delicious chunks from three swords and accepted two more; we were toasting each other in the cool Georgian wine; and I thought luncheon was done when in came a huge bowl of mutton soup, which perforce we spooned and sopped. Now, as we

were wiping the perspiration from our brows and about to sit back, in came the third course, a vast platter of pilaf. I groaned in protest, but again the chairman was breaking my bread for me; It would have been rude to refuse, so there was nothing for it but to accept the huge helping that came my way. Came a hint, too, for when I lifted my glass and proposed a toast to the blue trout of tomorrow, the Uzbek writer opposite me remarked casually that no fish had been taken from that stream in months. I wrote him off as one who didn't fish. But late that afternoon, Yuri, our interpreter, broke the news which my delegation hadn't the heart to tell me. "Your trip is off," he said. "I hate to disappoint you, but the guides have telephoned to say that the water is too low and that the trout have disappeared." (Was this true?) My face must have showed what I felt, for he added, "The chairman wants you all to dine with him tomorrow night, and he says you must bring your equipment and fish in the little river where the boys catch their carp." I had seen the little stream meandering through the city, the color of *café au lait* and almost as hot, but as this was a command performance, so be it.

Hamid's house was a new white frame three-story structure, rising high above the old town, and here at sunset we gathered, I with my rod and reel and flies. We were introduced to his oldest son of fifteen, and to his barefooted youngest of seven. Then we settled down to the fore part of the supper, the melons, the grapes, the toasts, and the first serving of lamb. An hour later I remarked to Hamid, "If I am to do any fishing this evening, someone will have to tie a rope around my ankle." Two hours later, while everyone watched, I set up the rod; I tied on a Mickey Finn as the one fly that might be seen in the murky depths, and then the seven-year-old, taking my hand, led the parade to the pool. Neighbors joined us from each doorway we passed, and we were a sizable procession by the time we reached the sluiceway, at the foot of which was a churning chocolate pool in which I was to cast.

The pool was thirty feet below us, but from where we were standing a path led to a parapet overhanging the water. At the base of it close to the water, a gardener with a spade had dug a little stand for me, while on the parapet overhead Turkish carpets had been laid, and here tea was served to the onlookers, to the Uzbek writers, and to the members of my delegation while I plied my darting fly through the muddy water. I had one strike — was it the bottom? — while Yuri kept advising: "They say the only way you will ever catch a fish here is to tie a stone on your line and use a worm." He was quite right.

When dusk fell we returned to Hamid's house, the seven-year-old now holding the fly rod in both hands before him like a standard. The walk had refreshed the taste buds, and Hamid's cousin had new steaming platters ready for us as we returned to the table. Of the toasts that followed, I remember one of Hamid's in the shank of the evening: "Here is to Mr. Weeks, who today has caught nothing but friends."

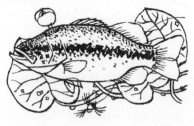

I was totally unprepared for the beauty of Slovenia, as indeed I was for so much of what happened to me in Yugoslavia. As a visiting editor in search of foreign contributors, I first presented my credentials in Belgrade, the national capital, beginning with a reception at our embassy, where I was introduced to a number of Yugoslav writers and critics. Then, as the nature of my mission became better understood by the Yugoslavs, the Ministry of Information came to my aid. They stocked my room with novels and with profusely illustrated art books in English translation; they set up for me the informal meetings I wanted in the world of art and education, and they made it clear that any *Atlantic* supplement which was to do justice to the country must include the writers and poets and painters of each of the six republics, small nations with vast cultural pride, which compose the state. This was to be a sensitive quest.

From Belgrade I headed north overland across the vast, well-cultivated Serbian plain for Zagreb and my long-promised meeting with Miroslav Krleza, the commanding Croatian novelist (had the Croatians the choice, they would have given him, not Andric, the Nobel Prize), and for my happy hours in the Zagreb studios and the beautiful century-old opera house. Then on to Ljubljana, which is the capital of Slovenia and the graphic arts, and the seat of some of the most fascinating discoveries in Illyrian and Centic archaelogy. All this while, I had been patiently trundling about my fly rod in its metal tube, and at last my Slovene friends arranged that I should have the chance to use it. A fishing license was procured for me at the Hunters Club, which had once been the resort of Viennese sportsmen. The bureaucrat, acting through my interpreter, gave me a permit for two days fishing on the Sava, the charge ten dollars a day in American currency.

"It's pretty early," I said. "Will they take a dry fly or a wet?"

"You're using flies?" (Evidently the spinning rod was a favorite.)

"Why, yes," I said.

"The charge will be five dollars a day."

Friends drove me up the valley that leads to Lake Bled and the foothills of the snowcapped Julian Alps — a landscape of timeless, breathtaking beauty with old castles or ruined country houses on the high points, cement pillboxes guarding every pass, and small shrines with fresh-cut flowers for the Partisans who had met their deaths here as they drove back the Italians and the Germans.

Tony, my weatherbeaten guide, spoke Slovene peppered with a few words common to all anglers. I had telephoned ahead that I hoped he could provide me with boots, and when he produced them, I knew I should be lucky if even one of them was dry, for they were multicolored with patches. In our Mercedes-Benz taxi, the status car in Yugoslavia, we then proceeded to the three miles of pools which only a desperate American would think of fishing as early in April as this. The Sava Bohinjka is a strong, deep stream, winding its way through the tiny alpine villages, through the deep woods and the sloping meadows with their Illyrian blue and banks of pink heather; a fine stream, and now in flood with the snow water pelting down from the

heights in an opaque green current so cool that it had driven the trout to the sunny shallows on either side. I was right about those boots. The right one was dry, the left leaked like a sieve, so I tried to do my casting from the starboard with my left foot on a rock or root. It didn't make much difference after the first ten minutes. My shin was so numb you could have hammered it without my feeling pain.

Because of the high water I had brought along my wet flies, and Tony would have none of them. "Fish take," he said disparagingly, shaking his head, "Tony give you vino." He watched patiently while I tried, and after twenty minutes with no follow, I thought I heard him murmuring, "Oh, Madonna! March Brown, March Brown."

"You got one?" I asked. He had, a March Brown dry; I put it on, and on the second cast a small trout in the shallows rose and took.

"Madonna, Madonna," said Tony. "Too small." All the rest of that afternoon till the light fell we worked our way along the bank, Tony scouting for the "big feesh" and I as patiently hooking the little ones. There is a twelve-inch limit on these streams, which were hard-hit and hand-grenaded for food by the Partisans during the war. Just before dark Tony came up with a tiny white moth. "You catch big feesh this, Tony get vino." I put it on; and then, seeing a good rise, we moved in its general direction, and the bit of white drifted in the widening ring. It was a good fish, as we saw when he turned and went down. Since I had no net, Tony, from the bank above me, kept shouting Slovene encouragement. With my dead left leg I moved into thinner water, and slowly, slowly worked the tiring Leviathan in. At that point the leader broke. "Madonna, Madonna!" groaned Tony. "No vino, no vino." But he got it anyway.

12. *THE BROAD SOUTHWEST*

I CAME to know Jack Russell in a literary way some
time before I had the pleasure of fishing with him on
the Southwest Miramichi. For two decades Jack and his
beautiful English wife, Jill, ran what was probably the
most popular, best-served salmon camp open to the public
in the Province of New Brunswick. My partner, Dick

Danielson, used to spend ten days there in early September in company with two quite famous Boston anglers, Richmond Fearing and Dr. "Chub" Newell, and he heard enough to believe that Jack had a remarkable story to tell and one that might do well in book form.

So one winter the author-to-be was installed in comfortable quarters in the Boston Tennis and Racquet Club and there through many a long day Jack puffed and glowered at a pad of yellow foolscap until he had produced a trial run of half a dozen chapters, which Dick read with dismay. They were an agglomeration of Canadian history, salmon genealogy and regulations for the care and feeding of "sports," authoritative but musclebound; Jack, who was a born raconteur, simply froze when he fingered the pencil. Yet at rare intervals a spark of humor or an episode told in the first person momentarily revealed the temper of the narrator and it was because of these clues that I was called in as the doctor.

Over drinks and through a leisurely dinner I realized that despite the written evidence Dick's confidence had not been misplaced. There was nothing taciturn about Jack Russell: he was a man of gusto, well compact, ruddy from his years on the river at all seasons, with strong expressive hands he radiated energy, and as he spoke and I saw the moods of reminiscence change from affection to scorn or indignation I was sure that he would be quick on the draw. A Canadian whose parents were living in Utah when he was born, Jack had the fearless temper of the West and it was one reason why the rivermen who built his cabins in the depth of the Depression stayed on to guide for him so loyally down the years.

Jack's life had been rejuvenated by the Atlantic salmon and this was the story on which he lifted the curtain that

evening and that had not been disclosed in the wooden para-
graphs. After an abortive start at Leland Stanford — his
freshman year lasted less than three months — he gravi-
tated to Detroit and into the motor industry in time to become a star salesman on a rising market: Fords, Stude-
bakers, Maxwells — he sold them all; his salesmanship took
him to Europe and to Russia just before the 1917 Revolution and after the war he was set up in London as the Eu-
ropean sales manager for Maxwell, where his success was
spectacular. He lived it up, he did not marry, nor did he
spare himself, and when at the height of the twenties he began to black out his doctor first warned him of his hyper-
tension and when this did no good told him frankly that if
he wanted to live he would have to give up his business and
go home. Jack, at forty-nine, wanted very much to live, for
he had fallen in love with Jill, a dark-eyed English bal-
lerina many years his junior; when they were married and
he had resigned his big salary, his worldly goods, give or
take a few thousand, depending on the stock market, centered in a fishing camp and 200 acres on East Musquash
Lake in northern Maine which became Jill's first home in
America.

Jack was an ardent and unorthodox angler who had
fished for trout in the Rockies and New Zealand and for
salmon in England, Scotland and Norway; his skill now
saved his bacon. A friend of his, drumming up publicity
for New Brunswick, asked him if he had ever killed a
salmon with a dry fly. Jack said no but he was sure he
could. A test match was arranged to take place on the magnificent Porter Cove Pool of the Southwest at Ludlow, pit-
ting Jack and his dry flies against an expert with the wet
fly, named James Briggs; each man was to fish for sixty
minutes, with reporters and a cameraman present to record

what happened. From the covered bridge that marks the eastern extremity of that great pool a cluster of mature fish and two grilse could plainly be seen and they were the target. Briggs went to work on them first with his two-handed rod and traditional equipment; he changed his wet flies frequently but though he stirred the fish he could not make one take. At last it was Jack's turn, and the guide spat with contempt when he saw how light was the rod, how small the dry fly. Jack began with a No. 10 Cow Dung, a tiny lure for a big fish, changed to an equally small Golden Ribbed Hare's Ear; and with it he lured and killed a grilse — at which the guide let out a war whoop! One by one, he rose, hooked and brought to the net the salmon in that pocket. "As far as I know," he said, "those were the first salmon that had ever been killed with a dry fly on the Miramichi." There was no one to dispute the claim and it put him in the headlines; his conquest was written up and talked about all over the north country, as it was for years to come at the Sportsmen's Shows in the States, with Jack on hand with pictures and leaflets to invite the inquisitive. Before he left Fredericton Jack had purchased the riparian rights on both sides of the Porter Cove Pool (a pool which in good water holds hundreds of fish and is spacious enough for four or more canoes). Then he went back to Maine to tell Jill of his new gamble.

This was the beginning of his second career, which still had to be written. From Jack's yellow pages we salvaged what we could for the *Atlantic* but the summer following, in mid-August when the guests were few, I went up to the Camp with Virginia Albee, my secretary, to have Jack talk his own story under my prodding while Jin took it down. I wanted Jill present at all our sessions and I asked Jack to call in his veterans who had retired, including Isabel, whose cooking had helped to give the place its reputation. They came, the rivermen, father and son; the Hoveys; the mainstays, Sharp Pond, Burt Pond and Billy Price (when the camp was built Billy would spear a good log and travel from Jack's camp site to his home four miles downriver, balancing on the log — and he couldn't swim a stroke); Marshall Blackmore, who stayed for eighteen years, and Fred Clowater, the gay one. Back they came, just as they had first come to Ludlow in the depths of the Depression, working for Jack at a dollar a day to build the cabins and, as time went on, to guide for Jack's guests. It was economy fishing at the outset: a cabin with plenty of hot water, delectable food, guide and canoe for ten dollars a rod a day! The rate was to go up, of course, but there were two rules which were never changed: a guide was forbidden to take a drink with a guest *on the river* (increasingly important as Jack acquired more pools further up and downstream), and, secondly, there was to be no fishing after supper. Jack had no wish to rescue a waterlogged martini drinker in the dark.

We toiled in one of the empty cabins from ten in the morning to five in the afternoon; the veterans visiting for a short piece to recall how things seemed from their end (in one of the first meals Jill cooked for the gang it was said that she managed to boil just enough potatoes for *one* ravenous man), but mostly it was Jack talking, Jill inserting and knitting, and I pelting along behind, questioning and rephrasing while somehow Jin got it all down, not of course in chronological order — that could be arranged later — but enough unadulterated Russell to compose ten chapters in ten consecutive days. This was the substance, amplified and published later, of Jack's book, *Jill and I and the Salmon,* which went through three printings. And incidentally, I always managed to get in an hour's fishing on the Home Pool in the early morning before the work began.

The Southwest Miramichi is a much broader, smoother-flowing stream than its northern brother and it attracts many thousands more salmon each year. The camp, full-blown, was drowsing in the August sun when I saw it. From the Newcastle road one approached across the water meadows and through a covered bridge, one hundred yards long, the place of the contest, a landmark for whose shade on hot days the big salmon would drift back from the home pool, to hold, fins and the big tails softly waving, cooling and communicating, if fish do, in the dark water. Between the cracks in the boards we would peer down, marveling at their size and beauty and knowing that no fly, could it be drifted over them in this slack current, would have the slightest effect.

Emerging from the gloom of the bridge one turned sharp right into Jack's drive which curved behind the five cabins on the river bank. ("The Five Little Cabins and How They Grew" was the first and facetious title.) Each had two double-bed rooms, a bathroom with shower, and a long living room opening on a porch, with a view up and down-stream, and of just the right size for neighborly cocktails. Within was a wood-fed stove for rainy days and at the rear, a boiler for hot water which could be stoked from the outside by a guide in the predawn without disturbing the sleepers within.

The bank on which the cabins poised was some twenty feet above the water level, not high enough, as it proved, to hold back the exceptional ice jam; spaced along it were small spruce to give shade to the porches and of just the right height for the drying of silk lines. At the end of the

row, directly above the canoe landing, was Jack and Jill's
house, in which they had braved their first Canadian winter
and in which Bill, their older son, had been born, to lord it
over young Jack who made a more protected debut in Connecticut two years later.

Here at small tables of a soft luster the community took
its meals and very good they were, for to Isabel's succulent
native dishes, the blueberry muffins, broiled grilse and
salmon chowder were added suggestions from the chef of
the Copley Plaza in Boston. The luster was Jill's accidental
addition, the olive oil with which she was rubbing baby Bill
overturned but gave to the wood such a pleasing glow that
it was applied to all the other tables. After dessert and
coffee one took one's ease in the living room which with its
open fire and memorabilia of other seasons, including the
silhouettes of two 25-pounders — big fish for the Southwest
— was an inviting place for good stories and rising hopes
for the morrow. Or one sat on the porch as dark fell watching the fireflies and the salmon moving on the surface or
perhaps spotting downstream the deer as they emerged from
that spring-fed backwater, the Bogan.

As we neared the close of the book a huskiness crept into
Jack's voice as he spoke of the old days of Billy Price and
Sharp Pond, the men who had meant so much to him, of
their sons who had taken their place and of Allen Hovey,
who had been killed overseas in the war. He knew as he approached seventy that the camp would have to pass into
younger hands: probably those of his able assistant, Eldred
Bailey; but he had made it, stamped it with his individu-
ality, and it had provided Jill and himself with twenty
years of happiness. We would stroll down to the bridge
where he would stand, gazing at the glorious, darkening
pool while he ruminated. I remember fragments: "In offer-

ing the dry fly I use an unorthodox method. I cast downstream not upstream, beginning close to the boat and letting the fly drift in long aisles toward the spot where I
know the fish are. . . . Here at the edge of this Home
Pool I erected a tower from which I could study the movement of the fish; in hot mornings they'd hold in those rocks
at the mouth of the Bogan where the cold water flows in.
I'd look right down on them and it was fascinating. . . .
I've had as many as twenty-four guides at one time working for me here. To relieve the pressure I'd take parties
far upriver to make the Half Moon trip in their canoes —
you'd like that — and while I was gone Jill ran the camp to
perfection. But I never could get her to fish when there were
any visitors around. . . . I can say in all sincerity that if
it hadn't been for the angling fraternity, there would be
few or no salmon left in the whole of Eastern Canada today. . . . In my twenty years on the river I have worked
harder to protect the salmon — against the set nets, the
poachers, the greedy trawlers in the Bay — than I have to
kill him. I wouldn't care if I never killed another."

"When did you begin to feel that way?" I asked.

"I guess it was when Ray Bergman was here," Jack continued. "We had some magnificent big trout in the Bogan then and the water was so still no one could touch them. Well, Ray went down one evening and captured the fly they were feeding on, had his wife tie one like it and then beckoned me to follow. On his knees in the tall grass he cast it out and let it sink. After a minute he began retrieving in short jerks and whango! What a beautiful fish! When the pool was calm again and he had dried the fly he repeated the operation and damned if he didn't get a second, just as big. Suddenly I got mad. 'Ray, you rascal, stop that!' I said, 'I don't want you to kill any more of those trout.' I guess that was the beginning."

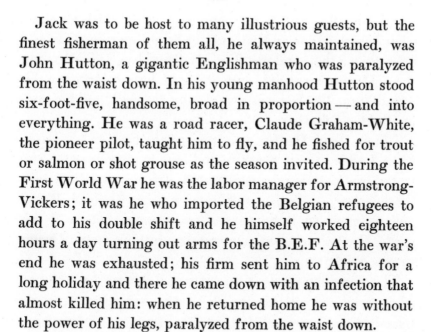

Jack was to be host to many illustrious guests, but the finest fisherman of them all, he always maintained, was John Hutton, a gigantic Englishman who was paralyzed from the waist down. In his young manhood Hutton stood six-foot-five, handsome, broad in proportion — and into everything. He was a road racer, Claude Graham-White, the pioneer pilot, taught him to fly, and he fished for trout or salmon or shot grouse as the season invited. During the First World War he was the labor manager for Armstrong-Vickers; it was he who imported the Belgian refugees to add to his double shift and he himself worked eighteen hours a day turning out arms for the B.E.F. At the war's end he was exhausted; his firm sent him to Africa for a long holiday and there he came down with an infection that almost killed him: when he returned home he was without the power of his legs, paralyzed from the waist down.

Fishing from a boat was the only pastime left him; with his pension he eked out an existence in the West Indies with just enough sterling to bring him to his best-beloved stream, the Southwest Miramichi, every other year. In camp his morning chemistry slowed him up and anyway his pride was such that he did not wish to be seen by the other guests, shuffling down, half supported by his guide, to the bow seat in the canoe. Patiently he waited until they were all on the stream and the morning was half gone; with his erect torso and wrists the size of two of mine there he would sit, being paddled out as the early birds, more rueful than not, were coming in with their catch. "Take my place on the Home Pool, Mr. Hutton," they would call to him. "I lost the only salmon I hooked," and in no time, in water that had been cast over and flogged for hours, he teased and killed an average of four salmon a day. Fred Clowater, his able guide, tells of the incredible deftness with which Hutton worked his fly, and of the confidence with which he chose what he was to use on that gray or bright morning. He had more than a thousand wet flies, small and large, chief among them Hutton's special, with its light blue coloring of his own design. The rod was dwarfed by his wrist, and his casting light as a feather.

I knew John Hutton only toward the close of his career when I added to his pleasure and ours by encouraging him to publish his reminiscences in the *Atlantic* and then take the next step — figuratively — of writing his book *Trout and Salmon*. In it he pays a conspicuous tribute to his guide, Fred, the esteem many anglers feel but do not always so generously convey.

The Canadian guide is a resourceful, taciturn woodsman whose relations with his "sport," as the visiting angler is referred to, are more subtle than meet the eye. Those of my generation were born in the settlements bordering the forest and got their initial training as lumbermen, cutting in the woods during the winter, and when the log drive was over in the spring, they turned to guiding, first the fishermen and then the hunters in the fall. They are expert in handling the axe or in poling a heavy canoe over rocks and through the strongest current. They all can cook the essentials, some of them very well; they can set up or take down a camp on short notice and they have the patience that comes from coping with all kinds of weather. As the forest was automated, the power saw, the Hyster, and the crane converted lumbering into a year-round occupation and the good guide became more of a rarity, better paid and better respected for the professional he is. The contamination of the streams in New England has made him one of a vanishing tribe there, but in Canada he is still to be relied on, for the law requires that any nonresident fishing or hunting in the forest must be accompanied by a registered guide. Incidentally, although most of them spend their lives on or near the water, few guides can swim.

Ostensibly what you pay your guide for is his knowledge of the river which he has acquired partly by inheritance and chiefly by his own prowess. Ranny Munn of Boiestown began guiding for Jack Russell in 1931, Jack's first year of operation; he was then twenty-two and when he was registered and received his badge his father, who had been guiding sports on the Southwest since the early 1890's, vouched for him. Jack put Ranny to work with the parties fishing their way downstream from Half Moon to the base camp at Ludlow, fifty miles as the crow flies but seeming a hundred as you paddle the winding stream. The parties — a guide to each canoe — and their duffle would go up by night train, be dumped off in the dark, catch what sleep they could in a ramshackle hut, and begin their trip with pancakes and coffee as the sun rose. To hurry is to miss the fishing and the wildlife: they would pause for a couple of days at Push and Be Damned — named for the rapids — with its fine pools, make another break at Clearwater or Burnt Hill and, coasting down through the wooded corridors of one of the loveliest unspoiled rivers in North America, be home in a week.

Accidents if they occurred were dealt with on the spot. My friend Hardwick Stires and his bride made the voyage on their honeymoon and, midway down, on her backcast she lodged her fly in her eyelid; with his thumb and forefinger he flicked the barb of the hook from the soft flesh without touching the eyeball; with her handkerchief she dabbed wet compresses until the stinging ceased, and was casting again by sunset. Surprises crop up, as when Matt White and I found awaiting us in an overnight cabin a bottle of Scotch and a sample dry fly (with a broken hook) thoughtfully left for us by Jim Babb, the Yale librarian, and his companion, who composed the party directly ahead. The liquor was most welcome as we were running low, so we finished off our own bottle and later, for a nightcap after an ice-cold shower, opened up our gift, only to find it was nothing but cold tea with the label neatly resealed over the cap.

But the fundamentals are the responsibility of the guide. From your bow seat as you watch a man like Ranny threading his way through the rapids, picking the surest path between the boulders with the white water pouring over them, is to be given a treat in canoe navigation. Or again in low water when he is bucking the current, you feel the power of his arms as his pole lifts the scraping boat over the thin channel. Ranny knows seventy miles of this river like the back of his hand: he knows the pools, great and small, and where the fish are likely to hold in June, in midsummer or

September; he knows the bars, the ledges and most important, when the water temperature is rising 70°; where the spring holes offer some refreshment and where the brooks flow in to those cooler spots that give the salmon anchorage.

The bigger the brook the finer the pool at its mouth. The famous ones on the upper reaches of the Southwest are: MacKeil Brook and McClean's; Burnt Hill Brook made famous by Jo Jefferson, the actor-angler, and Bliss Perry, the editor-angler; Clearwater Brook and Fistus; Rocky Brook and Salmon Brook, which I fish today as a guest of my friends Dale Furst and Bob DeVilbiss.

The clouds from the Bay of Fundy form the most glorious ramparts as evening approaches, great castellated masses of creamy white against the cerulean blue with undersides of mauve or dove gray. They can also settle down like a damp leaden curtain, emitting spurts of heavy rain and shutting out the sun for four or five successive days. At such times as the river rises and the fish, heedless now of the brooks, flee upstream, moving not in the turbulent current but close to the submerged shore, then Ranny becomes your man of hope. He knows the odds better than you do but in his taciturn way he keeps you trying: "I was fishing with Dale here last September and casting where you are he hooked into a nice salmon which we netted in the pool below." He knows as you do that September is the prime month on the Southwest when the water is cold, the foliage of the maple, oak and ash are turning, and salmon are pouring in from the sea; he knows that that fortunate time bears no relation to your present soggy dismay, that there is still the art of casting even over empty pools, and he must keep you at it.

A good guide, unlike the barber, is not out to flatter your

prejudices: in his laconic way he means to find out how much you know and then to help you where he can. The inexperienced will expect Ranny to pick the right fly, tie it on, and do half the casting. And not always the inexperienced: on the Restigouche I remember watching a club member seated with a backrest in the waist of the canoe while the guide in the bow scanned the pool and the guide in the stern did the casting; only when a fish had been hooked would the sport mark his place, close his book and take the rod. Well, that is certainly one way. But when Ranny is guiding for an angler who has fished elsewhere he accepts, even if he does not agree with, the other fellow's prerogative. I have occasionally overruled him and when I've been successful we both were pleased; when I was not he simply looks resigned, as if to say, "What could you expect?" But he does not say it.

Every self-respecting camp keeps a log in which such details as the weather and water temperature, the number and weight of the fish taken, who killed them and in what pool, are recorded. And when a guide has hooked the salmon or has ventured far out to release a line fouled up on a sunken log he should be credited. They know what we write about them but we do not know what they think about us, and I sometimes wish I were inside the sugar bowl on the guides' supper table to hear. Since they never boast of themselves I doubt if they boast of us. In the canoe they are invariably decent-spoken and only rarely does a story about the settlement reach our ears. I treasure one memorable bit that came to me, but not from Ranny. It concerns a big man in the community, physically big, whom we shall call Malcolm Macdonald, the father of several sons and two strapping daughters, the youngest of whom was unmarried and much sought-for. When the guide of her choice came to ask for her hand, old Malcolm who was hard of hearing thought he was asking for the loan of the family canoe, and he replied: "Well, you can have her, but you may want to bring her back. The boys have been dragging her back and forth over the rocks all summer and she's a little leaky in the stern."

Of the three Canadian rivers I have fished with intimacy, the broad Southwest is the only one to survive the foul-up of dams and pollution. At the Salmon Brook Camp three men provide for me as they do for my hosts, Ranny, Murray Calhoun, who outfits the camp and Kenny, his father-in-law, the neat and efficient cook; they are the human links reaching back to the days of Jack Russell and John Hutton and forward to next spring.

13. *WEST AND EAST*

I T is my experience that an Easterner is usually at a dis-
advantage when he goes fishing in the West, not because
he will seem a dude in their eyes but because he will rarely
have enough time to orient himself to the quite different
conditions. I dare say that the reverse is equally true and
that a master hand on the Eel or Rogue, two streams

famous for their steelhead, will feel strange when he first tries to cope with the Atlantic salmon. The solution in either case is to place yourself in the care of a native who is a good friend, borrow his flies, listen to his caution, and follow his example.

This is precisely what I tried to do when I had the opportunity of fishing for steelhead with Clark and Bill Van Fleet at the latter's ranch on the Klamath. The brothers are native sons of California. Bill, who is a veteran of the Lafayette Flying Corps in World War I, is short and sparky; Clark, the elder, is tall, blond and a very deft left-hander. They retired from the oil business in the late twenties and for three decades Bill's comfortable redwood house with its wide verandahs, set deep in a well-protected canyon below Orleans Bar, had been a fishing haven for both families. Bill's pools, covering close to a mile, were secured against interlopers by steep almost impenetrable slopes of Douglas fir on the eastern bank and by his own well-fenced farm on the west.

We began by eliminating my equipment. My old gray hat with a feather in it and my red-checked flannel shirt were the only distinguishing bits I was permitted to wear. My felt-soled waders were ruled out as being too soft. "You need leather boots with steel brads and well protected toes for the algae-covered boulders in the Klamath," said Bill, "and for your breast-high waders you ought to have a marine belt, strapped under the arms to keep the water out when you fall in. As you will." With docility I was fitted into this underwater suit. "When you fall," he continued, "try to fall sideways, holding your rod up. If you fall straight ahead, there's the danger that the current will continue to roll you over." My rod was discarded as too short and my flies, of course, were foreign.

The steelhead is a rainbow trout who like the Atlantic salmon goes to sea for his growth, back to his home river to spawn, and then to sea again if he can make it. He has been doing this since time immemorial and his size and speed make him the finest freshwater character on the Pacific coast. Also quite the best to eat. One casts for the steelhead as deep in the river as one dares, facing downstream and in ever-widening arcs. The moment of truth is apt to occur when the line has straightened out and then even a short twitch of the fly may bring an explosion. The fish is likely to take off downstream, the reel screaming, the angler bucking for shallower water, stumbling and stubbing over some of the roundest and slipperiest rocks on any river bottom. When you catch up with your fish and play him out he is either beached or booted ashore, depending on his size.

It may be wondered why with all this adversity one has to venture so deep and the answer is simple — that is where the bigger fish lie. So you sidle out crabstyle bracing yourself against the current until you have the sensation of sitting on it. Yes, but the large rings are still deeper, beyond your furthest cast, so cautiously on you go, the water level rising above your belly and your heels as your last checkpoint; but just as you notice that the rocks in the center feel smaller, like scree on a mountainside, they all begin to slide and you with them; you turn on your side and your free arm plunges shoulder-deep in the cold water as you scrabble to right yourself.

I followed the predictions as reasonably as I could and

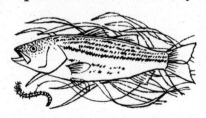

my behavior, witnessed by Bill's neighbor who was fishing above us, when reported to the brothers was evidently reassuring. The marine belt had kept the water out of me except for a mild sensation in the left leg.

In every river heaven there is a Lucifer and in Bill Van Fleet's it was the hydroelectric power company, a hundred miles or so upstream, which had altered things greatly since the halcyon days by its daily process of "bumping" the water, releasing it, then stopping the flow, then releasing it again after a couple of hours: the effect of this ever-changing water level was to speed up the incoming steelheads; instead of pooling up overnight as they had in the past, they charged straight through to their spawning beds with only a minimum tarry in the deepest spots. As a concession to the anglers the power company agreed to do no bumping on Sundays. At our distance from the dam this meant that the river would begin to smooth out after midnight and that Monday morning would be our best chance.

Monday morning at 2:45 Bill, Clark, their nephew and I were alerted by the alarm clock and the girls, bless them, saw that we had a stout breakfast and thermos and sandwiches for the car; we drove like the wind to a wider, deeper gorge, parked, and were picking our way down the canyon wall with our flash torches when the next carful with the same thought in mind came up the road with its headlights drilling the dark. As firstcomers we had the prime position and in our waders we took up our stations thirty yards apart, I closest to the rapids in the gorge, the other three in a file behind, and behind them the second party was getting set. Canyon fishing is a noisy affair. "Fish carefully," shouted Bill, "and then move down a little." I did as bid and got a good strike as my line straightened out near a half-submerged rock. Bill, who was watching, let out a war whoop.

"Get the hell out of there!" he yelled. "Beach your fish and let a man in!" The steelhead was well hooked — as he needed to be in my corkscrew passage over those boulders — and at the end a mild dropkick got him to the sand. He looked to be about 4 pounds, the sheen in his silver body already beginning to fade. After a nip of coffee and retying my fly I plowed in at the end of our file and had the fun of watching the others as I fished.

We all caught and with beginner's luck, I the biggest. This would not have been so had Clark been able to hold the steelhead that took at the same rock I had been aiming for and then sped like light into the rapids. Clark galloped after him and it was amazing to see his tall rangy figure navigate in those perilous waters. He disappeared from sight, Bill whooping encouragement but when he reappeared there was no fish dangling from the cord on his belt.

Patsy, Bill's wife, broiled our catch for supper, the red flesh of the steelhead, juicy and delectable. In the leisurely cocktail hour on the porch with a new moon hanging over the pass, there was a brief ceremony in which the editor was presented with a medal, a half-dollar, circa 1928, set in a copper frame with a purple velvet ribbon into which had been sewn a four-leaf clover in tiny beads and a Royal Coachman trout fly. The trophy had been held by whichever brother was top rod; now it was mine, one of the bits of memorabilia which my grandson David has not yet been permitted to confiscate. Through the evening, as the brothers talked of their early days on the Mackenzie, the Eel and the Rogue, I realized I was hearing the source material for a book, and indeed I was; it appeared a year later under the Atlantic–Little, Brown imprint: *Steelhead to a Fly* by Clark Van Fleet.

My speaking trips to the Coast occurred periodically and I could tell in advance when there was likely to be a respite for fishing. At the University of Oregon the program chairman, himself an angler, advised me to drop off the train at Roseburg the night before my talk; there he and the chairman of the English Department would meet me and we would spend the sunrise hours on the Umpqua River the next morning and still make the campus in good time for my lecture. Things worked out well: with borrowed gear and an expert boatman I caught two silverside salmon, the larger 18 pounds, and was of course photographed with them just before I headed for the auditorium.

Sometimes Fritzy and I foraged for ourselves. My lecture at the University of Idaho was over at noon and a bright October weekend stretched ahead until my next engagement Monday evening. I flew to Spokane, picked up my partner and before renting a car paused at a tackle shop to get our licenses and advice.

The proprietor looked me over quizzically."We close our camps earlier than you people back East," he said, "but young Elkins has some fine cabins up on Priest Lake and if he'll take you in you'll see plenty of cutthroat and some fine country."

We figured I should be able to get there for supper but I missed a couple of turns and it was dark and cool before I found the Elkins entrance, coasted up to the main cabin and switched off the headlights. In the large cosy kitchen Elkins and the housekeeper had finished their meal; Dusty the Labrador rose to meet us and the big tomcat lay fast asleep on the open oven door. We were as welcome as an attack of measles.

"I can't turn you away at this hour," said the hefty proprietor, "but this camp is *closed*. My housekeeper has been ironing the curtains for the next season and I'm repainting the boats. We'll give you some ham sandwiches and coffee and put you up on cots for tonight. But that's it." We were properly abashed.

But at breakfast Elkins, who proved to be more likable by the minute, had relented. They would take us if we ate with them and asked no favors. A cabin on the bluff, overlooking the lake, but not yet dismantled, was to be ours till Monday noon. "As for the fishing," said Elkins, "they'll be as many cutthroat feeding in our cove as anywhere else in the lake and that way you won't have to fuss with an outboard." Horses and outboards are adjuncts to fishing I like to do without, so I was delighted at the prospect. "If you want to see how big they get look through the cracks in the dock until you spot our mascot." I did and when I spotted him I was goggle-eyed; he was a hugie, with the scarlet diagonals clearly to be seen either side of his fat throat. Most camps have a pet fish who dwells in the shade of the landing and is so well fed he resists any lure.

So began one of those brief interludes when confidences come easily and the interchange makes for swift friendliness. While the housekeeper washed and ironed, Elkins painted his boats listening to the World Series which came to his transistor from Yankee Stadium, and I rowed our ponderous skiff in slow circles around our cove. The cutthroat feeds as he goes, in a straight line which one can perceive on the surface, and the art is to place your dry fly directly ahead of his arrow and hit him when he sucks it down. We netted just enough for supper and Fritzy, trolling, picked up a couple of small silversides, salmon pink and equally delicious. When we weren't studying the water we were resting our eyes on the Coeur d'Alene, that vast enclosing ring of rugged slopes, some heavily wooded, some burned to the rock by the forest fires that ravaged this country decades ago. The mountains to the northeast were denuded and we wondered if the growth would ever be restored and why the flames stopped where they did. Probably the wind shifted, and the rains came.

On this particular trip a still greater surprise awaited me at the University of Washington in Seattle. I had been asked if I would meet the press at the Fisheries Center in advance of my lectures and I was totally unprepared for such a large modern laboratory, on the lower slope of the campus a stone's throw from Portage Bay with such a professional corps dedicated to the fertilization, rearing, and preservation of the Pacific salmon and other freshwater fish. My interviews were conducted in the auditorium, in that moist fishy atmosphere dear to every angler, and when they were over one of the professors, Dr. Lauren R. Donaldson, introduced me to members of his staff and some of his students, who have been carrying on experiments in the breeding and rearing of Chinook salmon, steelhead, and rainbow trout, experiments which have had a revitalizing effect on rivers the world over.

For over thirty years, Dr. Donaldson has been giving thought to the development of "super salmon" by selective breeding, and when the center was established in 1949 he had a school of what he believed would be particularly hardy fingerlings ready to release from the laboratory pools. A fish ladder with four steps led from cement pools into Portage Bay, and down went the fingerlings, through the Bay, through Lake Union, through the locks of a government canal, through Puget Sound, and out into the Pacific. Normally about one tenth of one per cent of naturally bred salmon return to their spawning grounds in a matter of four years. The question involved in "Donaldson's folly," as campus critics called it, was how many — if any — of the University reared and marked fingerlings would return, and when.

It must have been a tense moment when, in 1951, the first homing Chinook swirled and began his leaping, slithering ascent up the ladder with its foot-wide openings. "We waited and waited," said the doctor. "Finally, they started coming in. They were little runts, but they had our brand on them, and I could have kissed each one of them." Not so little, either, for they averaged 18 pounds, a growth they had attained in just under three years.

Four came back from that first trial; 48 in 1955; in 1959, 872, and now 3000 or more return each fall. Were this to continue unchecked, the university would be overrun with salmon, for this is a fish story to put "Pigs Is Pigs," Ellis Parker Butler's classic, in the shade. What Dr. Donaldson and his team are doing is stripping the eggs from the returnees and again, after selective breeding and rearing, releasing the hardiest fingerlings from a small pond that has been built on the campus, whose waters flow into the Pacific. A quarter-million go out to sea annually, and some five million pedigreed eggs are available for state hatcheries and fish farms. Studies thus far indicate a rate of 60 per cent survival in the University ponds, with at least 10 per cent survival in the deep sea. If six million of these selected fingerlings can be released, that could mean a return of 600,000 Chinooks for sports and commercial fishermen — and propagation. To simplify the statistics Dr. Donaldson wrote down on a paper towel for me, a decade of testing has shown that thirty times as many college-bred salmon return home to spawn as noncollegiate.

What about their diet? The main laboratory, whose doors open onto the college pools, encloses two rows of large tanks, each cared for by a pair of students in their rubber aprons and boots. The fingerlings were being measured for growth at the time of my visit, and eager, observant faces — American, Filipino, Thai, and Japanese — were studying the slender glass tubes through which the silver streaks were being poured. Dr. Donaldson is an authority on radiation biology, and his research on the results of the nuclear explosions in the Pacific has taught him that certain minerals, such as iodine, zinc, cobalt iron, and manganese, contribute to a fish's growth — a peaceful byproduct of a dreadful accident, the fallout which endangered the lives of Japanese commercial fishermen. His experiments are calculated to make up the deficiencies in such minerals in lakes and streams now being tested for new fish populations.

The fish pens next to the college salmon pools are reserved for the nontravelers, the home-bred rainbow trout. I looked down on their broad black backs in amazement for I had never seen rainbows so big. "Lord, what do those giants weigh?" I asked.

"Oh, ten or eleven pounds," the doctor replied. "We'll net one for you." And when we returned to the laboratory, there he was, Big Sulky, in a tank by himself, levitating, puffing in his anger at having been abducted, the red flush big as a rose beneath his eye and the exquisite rainbow coloring all along his broad beam. "Eleven pounds," said the doctor, "and he's just two years old."

"What'll you do with him?"

"We release these trout in some of the nearby lakes," he said, and added reflectively, "I generally know where they've been put, and sometimes at dusk I drive out and watch the fun. Pretty soon I'll hear a man shout, 'Brother, I'm into a biggy. Wow, watch him go!' Great excitement for a minute and a half, then silence . . . 'Gee, he stripped me clean!' "

"I guess you were cheering for the fish," I said.

At a time when fresh waters in the United States are contaminated the country over with the resulting destruction of fish life, and when far, far too many of our salt marshes along the Atlantic seaboard on which crustacean and school fish depend for their sustenance have been filled in by the hit-and-run contractor, it was enormously heartening to hear that such a positive program for the selective breeding of salmonoid fishes had been generated on the Pacific Coast, where the population pressure grows ever more intense.

In the years since my first visit the news about the research carried on at the Fisheries Center in Seattle has traveled far: students from thirty-six nations, thirteen of them in the Pacific, have come to study at the Center, clear recognition of how many foreign governments are now concerned about their future source of supply. That the fish diets and the crossbreeding approved by Donaldson's team can build up local stocks in such short time is knowledge indispensable to countries like India, Pakistan, Malaysia, and Japan. Faculty members from the Center have taken sabbatical leave to serve as consultants in Germany, Kenya, Italy, and in South America, and it is significant that Professor Donald E. Bevan and Professor Ule Mathiesen have spent collectively over two years teaching and expounding in the Soviet Union. The nature of the new experimentation for American purposes is projected, I think with some excitement, in Dr. Donaldson's letter to me of June 13, 1967:

We are especially pleased with the interracial hybrid we have created by crossing our select stock of rainbows with the migratory strain of rainbows (steelhead). These fish have the good characteristics of both parent strains. They grow more rapidly and reach smolt size in 4 to 6 months, instead of the 2 years (plus or minus) for the steelhead strain. They do not grow as fast as the rainbow strain but do migrate to sea and "home" to the pond on the campus. Fortunately for the anglers, they bite on various lures much more energetically than do the steelhead. This characteristic is a very useful one in our management scheme for we do not wish to have the fish return for use as brood stock. At the present state of our knowledge we think it is better to make the cross each year and have the fish completely harvested upon their return from the sea. Thus we have complete control of the stock and can keep constantly improving the quality.

A lecturer learns by listening. It was in the mountain states of Arizona and Colorado that the truth of the water shortage really came home to me. At Tempe, Arizona, where I addressed the State University, the president startled me when he said, "We're mining water here. The water table has dropped fourteen feet in the past ten years. We are beginning to realize that we'll have water enough for more cattle and vegetables, or for more people. Not for both."

California, which is growing faster than any state in the union, is squarely up against this hard reality, and in desperation the golden bear has been levying claims on rivers whose headquarters are in neighboring states. I listened to heated discussions of the water war when I was speaking at the Aspen Institute in Colorado (with a little fishing in C. R. Smith's cold trout stream to calm my mind). What I was hearing, of course, were the first stages of a national crisis which, when drought sharpened the emergency, could affect that watery paradise the Everglades just as swiftly as it did the Rockies and the driest of our mountain areas. California not only needs more water, it needs more electric power for the new homes, and the repeated damming of its fine rivers has done away with its anadromous fish like the steelhead. The pollution and the dead water shut them off from any possibility of leaving their spawning beds, and they have ceased to return. This has another hard consequence since it diverts to the still clear streams in the Northwest the hordes of California fishermen who no longer have the sport they want at home.

Year by year the good rivers are harder hit and I saw how true this was on my repeated visits further inland, when I taught at the Writers' Conference at the University of Colorado. Here I fished in the company of my niece, Betty Cross, and her talented, artistic husband Gerry; Betty ought to write a cookbook about picnic lunches so unusually good they are, and as for Gerry, when he is not painting or teaching, he is scouting for a pond, a lake, or a stream which holds trout and is so hard to get to that only a few will take the trouble. In my rubber pants and with my breath coming shorter I have climbed the last thousand feet up the trail to Mitchell Lake for the cutthroats which, in one of those heavenly hours when the wind isn't blowing, will be feeding on the surface. At 11,000 feet Mitchell is half above the tree line and there is nothing to stop the gigantic gusts which with no warning sweep down from the snow-clad peaks. It is the most picturesque small body of water I have ever fished, with a glacial pit in the center from which the cutthroat emerge to feed along the bar.

Happily for me my travels took me to the Campbell River on the island of Vancouver there to stay with a writer, Roderick Haig-Brown, whom I had heard lecture in the East and who epitomizes better than any other I know the evolution of a two-fisted hunter and fisherman into a thoughful, two-fisted leader in conservation. Rod, who is English-born, has very dark eyes and hair as black as a raven; his frame is long, lean and tireless, as I know from trying to follow him in waders over and under the Douglas fir slash that littered a shoreline, and he has the poise and competence of a fine woodsman which he acquired early in life. His family had intended him for the Civil Service, but he finished school at seventeen and it seemed a good idea to farm him out with a relative who owned a logging operation on the shores of Lake Cavanaugh in Washington. A year or so in the Northwest might fill him out.

His first job was scaling logs behind contract fallers — and it was well to do right by the fallers or they might drop a tree on you; after three months of this he worked on the rigging of the famous Washington Flyer, a giant skidding machine, and thence he was transferred to a survey crew mapping, bridging and laying out a railroad. Evenings after work, he who had always loved fishing had his first encounters with steelhead, Dolly Vardens and cutthroat. Rod had entered the United States as a student and when his year was up he headed north into the Nimpkish country on Northern Vancouver Island; he was on his own, cruising timber, repairing telephone lines, fishing in the fall for tyees and cohos salmon which he sold for ten to twelve cents a pound, and through the winter running a registered trapline on the Kilipi River. When he was twenty-one, with cash in his pocket, he returned as promised to England, and on the way back at Seattle he met Ann, an honors student at Berkeley; they got along well but briefly and at the time she thought him excessively youthful.

Back in England he found that the requirements for the Colonial Civil Service had changed under the secretaryship of Sidney Webb: only university graduates need apply and Rod was a working man. Over the protests of his family he began free-lancing in London: he had sold his first pieces to the *Fishing Gazette* and other sporting magazines from the time he was in school; now he wrote for anything and everything that would pay him a guinea, worked as a film extra, advised on outdoor scenes, and worked on his books. He had two sources of material to draw on: the trout and salmon streams of Britain and the wilderness of the Northwest. *Silver,* his first book, was accepted in 1931 and *Pool and Rapid* had been drafted when his heart decided that it would be more fun to buck the Depression in Vancouver than in London. The winter of 1932–33 while he was waiting for his books to pan out he became very interested in cougars and the whole of that winter he hunted with the famous "Cougar" Smith. And at Christmastime he came out of the woods and hunted for Ann: they were married in Seattle in January 1934 and moved up to pioneer in Campbell River a month later.

Campbell River was then a settlement of some five hundred people at the end of the road on Vancouver Island, but there was a road, a school and a hospital — and in the river, the bravest and wiliest of all Pacific fish, the steelhead. It was a startling change for Ann, who was city-bred: no electric power, wood stove, milk from the cow, eggs from *their* chickens, vegetables from a garden Rod didn't know how to grow, water in uncertain supply from a crazy pump in the river. They began in a rented house but in 1936, pooling all savings and credit, they bought twenty acres on the west bank, just above tidewater, and built their own dwelling to be enlarged as books and the children came. Their oldest daughter, Valerie, was the first child to complete all twelve grades in the Campbell River School (when young Alan and the other girls came along, this was not so much of a feat) and when in 1947 Rod, drawing on his veteran's credit, built the Big Room with its open fire, books to the ceiling and the broad desk by the western window, as soundproof as Ann could make it, he at last had a place where he could write with continuity.

The most lyrical of Rod's works in this period is *A River Never Sleeps,* in which he blends the observation and adventure of his boyhood in England, when he was eager for all manner of fish, with what he had come to learn in action and reflection in the Northwest. There was a guidebook, *That Other Trout Season* published by Pan American Airways, in which he writes of the hospitable mountain folk of Chile and the tests he made with dry fly and light tackle in those lakes and mountain torrents where our rainbow trout have grown to such size. There were the four books on the seasons beginning with *Fisherman's Spring* and ending with *Fisherman's Fall,* in which he savors and spells out the seasonal effect on the comings and goings of the steelhead at his back door. And, remarkable in summing up his transition, there is *The Living Land* with its two-year, unsparing, farsighted survey of the forests, streams, wildlife, pollution, and the government's attitude toward the same in British Columbia, which he wrote on a grant from the British Columbia Resources Conference. His findings did not endear him to the authorities.

Rod and Ann have helped build their community. A share of their twenty acres they gave as the site for the new church. Ann serves as librarian in the senior high school;

Rod's duties as magistrate and in the Family Court, his work as consultant for the new aquarium for Vancouver, his year-long service on the Federal reapportionment commission, his outspoken talks on conservation mark the growth of his public spirit. Ann concedes that "he has grown up a lot."

Rod's pools hold just as many fish as ever but he would as soon explore them today in wet suit, snorkel, with underwater camera as with a fly. During my visit we made an 120-mile foray deep into a superb forest of first-growth Douglas fir; passing, if I counted correctly, through seven gates before we reached the Gold River which was taking in the spring run of steelhead. We were four, the two of us, Rod's old friend "Skate" Hames, the cougar hunter and conservation officer, and Maxine, a willowy blonde, wife of the biology teacher at the High School, who always went along with her husband, but this time he was tied up. I remember the eagle, the two black bear working over the dump, and the innumerable elk, the bulls, fat brown blobs in the uplands, sensitive of their new horns, the does and young browsing at the water's edge. I remember how drenchingly it rained throughout the first day, how rugged the wading and how painful the feet when socks inside the boots became wet and chafing. But the moon rode clear

after our supper at the logging camp — a supper warmed
for us all by Rod's flask of rum — and the next morning
we fished under a bright sun in full sight of the snowclad
peaks. Rod the purist used wet flies and so did I the first
day and drew a blank — then I appropriated the lion
hunter's spinning rod until my tally included a 9-pounder.
Maxine was also spinning, casting sixty, seventy feet with
salmon eggs for her lure. In all we hooked 19 steelhead,
kept 6, lost 6, and returned 7, kelts, fish that had spawned
and were returning to the sea. Of our keep, the largest
weighed just over 13 pounds.

I remember that the talk on the long ride home came
to pollution and settled there; pollution of the air in our
cities, of the land by pesticides, and pollution of our
streams, and Rod's saying that all pollution is the use of
public property for private profit. It takes many forms,
he said, but pollution is always detectable and most accurately measured at its source. Let's put a graduated tax on
pollution now; begin low and work up to maximum elimi-
nation before the mess gets worse.

Rod has been extending his influence recently through
the films he has been making, one called *Fisherman's Fall*
for the National Film Board and a much more ambitious
project showing the artificial spawning beds and the better
distribution of young fish which is being attempted in the
Babine Lake Salmon Project. But he is first and last a
writer and when I prod him, as I do occasionally from
Boston, to put his philosophy into words, this is what I get
by return mail:

I think of myself as a writer, not a conservationist, and I think
of conservation in terms of all natural resources, because their uses
are substantially interdependent, and I believe the first essential is
basic knowledge of how and why things work and interact, so that

man can work in harmony with the revealed patterns, not against them. I believe devoutly in the possibilities of and the need for habitat improvement in lakes, streams, estuaries and salt water and am intent on such ideas, for instance, as the improvement and enlargement of spawning areas and nursing areas.

I believe the North American continent has need of a new ideal man. In place of the aggressive, pragmatic, ruthless developer who was needed to open up the continent, we now have need of a much gentler, more generous and sensitive individual, far more sophisticated and no less able, who is fit to understand and use and preserve an opened continent. I used to think it would be necessary to create this ideal by all the means of advertising, education and propaganda, to say nothing of religion, that was used to produce the old ideal. I no longer think so. I believe it already exists in the young people of to-day and needs only to be recognised and put to use.

14. *DAM THE TOBIQUE*

O NE of the compensations of growing older is to
join with friends who are finding in nature what
they had never found in the more competitive sports of
their youth. In the early 1950's three of my contemporaries
— Charles S. Gage, the Treasurer of Yale, J. Mattocks
White, who had been in the class behind him at New

Haven, and J. Hampden Robb, the Boston architect — formed a syndicate to buy the modest salmon camp on the Tobique which for many years had been the summer haven of J. Kenly Bacon, a former member of the State Department. I use "modest" to describe the six pools whose lease they purchased, for these were "hurrying pools." I mean the fish sped into them and tarried but briefly before hurrying out again. "Ken" Bacon's property at Riley Brook, which had been christened Deer Point, was actually a small centerpiece separating the lower camp and the richly productive waters of the Tobique Salmon Club from its upper camp with the magnificent chain of pools formed by the confluence of several streams at the Forks. Once they reached the Forks the fish stayed put for days before continuing up into the headwaters of their destined rivers: the Little Tobique, the Serpentine, the Campbell, the Sisson and the Mamozekel. The Tobique, which is the main tributary of the St. John, had an annual inflow of some 7000 salmon and grilse; this was approximately the number that was counted the first year the salmon had worked their way through the fish ladder, the series of connecting cement pools, which carried them up and over the dam at Perth, where the Tobique and the St. John divide. At one time or another, every one of those fish — save those killed by the Club members — had to pass Deer Point on their way to the spawning beds. It seemed like a good place to be.

The camp — or camps, for there were two of them — sat on a high bluff, facing upstream, separated by twenty yards of greensward and identical in every detail. They were a promoter's dream of what a fishing camp should look like; a living room two stories high with an enormous fireplace, a curving stairway leading up to a romantic nook under the eaves (where the liquor was stored) and the walls covered with African spears and quite fine heads of elk, moose, buffalo, mountain lion, and mountain goat, the lot, I suspect, having been picked up cheap from a Broadway taxidermist. The original owners made their money in Florida real estate and lost it as quickly; after the crash the camps passed to a beneficent old party who amused himself by entertaining Lolitas and breeding pigeons, and thence into the hands of Ken Bacon, who was the first to fish from them vigilantly. For his guide and caretaker he acquired the services of John Parrish, a shrewd, wiry native, not much given to words but when he spoke, decisive. Here each summer on his month's holiday from foreign service Ken, his wife and John were like hawks in their devotion to the river. Through the opening in the trees, carefully cut by John, they could see if salmon were moving on the surface of either the Slough or the Bogan, the two best pools — and if they were, either water could be reached in six minutes. Ken taught his German shepherd to watch from the bluff for signs of a jumping fish; when he heard the bark Ken trained his binoculars upstream and called John. He had John build a watertight rock pool in the shade of the drive and keep it fresh with river water so that he could closely observe for a couple of days the fish they had brought home alive. When the salmon began to weaken he netted them and gave them back their freedom. He lived, ate and dreamt of fish.

In good years Ken's log showed a take of 40 salmon and grilse, a vigilant performance for two rods in a month. But this had been in the halcyon days before the erection of the hydroelectric dam at Perth, and Ken's successors were naturally curious to see what difference it might make to their newly acquired pools. So was the Commissioner of

Land and Mines, who is responsible for the protection of wildlife in the province. Salmon which since time prehistoric had encountered no worse obstruction than fish nets on their way upstream do not take readily to an artificial fish ladder; they have to be persuaded that it is the only way, and while they are milling about at the foot of the dam making up their minds, they have to be protected from the horde of fishermen who would be casting over them in their vulnerable state if the law did not prohibit. There was also the problem of holding and counting them in the big fish box at the top of the ladder, which for a wild thing is almost unendurable. Finally, any dam of size backs up a deep, fat stretch of water with very little current for miles — while a salmon is bred and shaped to fight the strongest water. Would they make it or would the run decline?

The Boston proprietors, Matt White and Ham Robb, invited me to join them on their first spring visit to Riley Brook and for our fourth we had Horace W. Cole, Yale athlete and State Street banker who like all of us had taken to fishing in his later years. On the drive up I am not sure it was not Ham who observed how very attractive the Canadian girls looked the moment we crossed the border. The truth of this has come back to me often and it is not just the muskiness of males away from home; the girls, many of Scotch heritage and coloring, are comely, and since the road is their chief promenade and since they enjoy attention as much as any on Fifth Avenue and, thanks to the shopping center, can dress for it no less invitingly, there is no doubt that on the wing they do distract the mind.

When we stopped at Perth, however, it was not for dalliance but to inspect the fish ladder at the new dam and to get the score of how many had passed up it. About the latter the custodian was evasive. He left the impression of several hundred but was more specific about the last two days when he said thirty-five had been counted through the box, most of them mature fish. We could see for ourselves that others were on the way. It is roughly seventy feet from the floor of the river to the top of the dam and to make that ascent the fish were battling their way up a serpentine of thirty connecting cement compartments, each ten feet square, through which the water rushed with heavy momentum. The walls were four and a half feet high, so we could peer into the compartments nearing the summit and count, here a grilse, there two salmon — and everywhere, adhering to the fish or the concrete, the lamprey eels. The lampreys are parasites with an affinity for salmon and you will often notice the small circular scar in the salmon's side where an eel has applied his suction. I once hooked a salmon with the lamprey still attached and saw with what loathing the guide stamped the eel into the earth. On this day two men with pitchforks were employed in spooning the lampreys out of the compartments, and there by the side of the serpentine they lay in heaps — "good for nothin' else but fertilizer" as one of the pitchforkers remarked.

John Parrish and his elderly neighbor Austin Hubbard, who would be guiding in our two canoes, were at the camp to greet us and help unpack. John is not exactly an optimist — he could never forget the unfettered days with Ken Bacon and he had a hearty distrust of the dam — but he brightened our hopes by reporting that club members had killed two salmon in the pools directly below us the evening before, and, as a token of confidence, I noticed he had filled the reservoir in the drive with river water in the event that we hooked enough fish to bring one back alive.

[*197*]

We had arrived firm in the resolve to live by a do-it-yourself regime. Hoddy Cole liked to cook and was good at it, so that was taken care of, and the bedmaking and cleaning-up could be fitted in when we weren't fishing. Fine in theory but as it proved the grunt work and the amenities both consumed a good deal more time than we allowed for on the drive up. Here was the way things worked out:

DEER POINT TIMETABLE

7 A.M. Camp awakes. After shaving Cole starts the coffee, bacon and pancake batter

8 A.M. Breakfast, followed by allocation of pools (we fished two men to a boat and in rotation, 20 minutes of casting or a fish, parr not counting)

1 P.M. Boats return

1:15–2 P.M. Cocktails, sporadic washing of breakfast dishes, followed by light lunch

2–3:30 P.M. Naps, bedmaking, greasing lines, exchanging flies and advice

4:30–9:30 P.M. Evening fishing

9:30–10:30 P.M. Martinis and trout à la Weeks

10:30–11 P.M. Dinner — or later if cook has been distracted by cocktail banter

Midnight–Washing-up. (How could there be so many dishes?)

12:30–1:30 Bull session and nightcaps on porch

After five days of this we began to realize that women did have a place in a man's world even in a fishing camp. Things were brought to a head by Ham Robb, who, perhaps as a gentle reproach, recalled how he had once fished in style at the Pulitzers' camp on the Restigouche. "We never went out on the water till eleven-thirty in the morning," he said, "had our cocktails and luncheon at four; rested till the evening fishing which began at six-thirty, and came in at dark to dress for dinner. The chef and the

champagne were excellent." The only moral to be drawn
was that our own chef needed relief. He spent too much
time over that wood stove. If he took his cocktail with him
into the kitchen it grew warm. If he was attracted to the
porch for a refill and to hear what we were laughing at, the
fire went out. The best compromise we could think of was to
move the hot meal to noon and do all the washing before we
collapsed for our naps (not till the next year did it occur to
us to hire a cook).

But the tedium of doing for ourselves was as nothing
compared to our disappointment on the water. Five bright,
hot days passed in succession as the river dropped lower
and lower. Each morning we would descend the dew-
dampened path full of hope and at day's end climb back
up it through the spruce, empty-handed or at best with a
couple of trout. We occasionally saw salmon in our pools
and at long intervals managed to raise one. Matt, fishing
the Island pool late one evening, raised a good fish with his
Nighthawk but it struck just as Matt was beginning to retrieve and never came back. Ham, who cast a very long
line, had a special attraction for the river chub, big stolid
ones which put up such a fuss you might have thought
he had tied into something keepable. One afternoon John
dug up some garden worms. We shifted to small hooks and
went up to a couple of potholes in slack water where we
hauled in a fine mess of trout for supper, the more delicious
for the fiddlehead salad which Austie's wife sent over to us.
And I made regular forays up Riley Brook for the sweet
little brookies which were our hors d'oeuvres. But by the
evening of our sixth day when we had again drawn a complete blank in salmon it seemed conclusive that there were
fewer fish in the river than ever in years before and that
we'd better close up shop.

That evening Ham and I were sharing a rod with Austie
as our guide. As he lined us up and dropped his killick in
the Bogan Pool a small salmon came clear out of water.
This is not a long pool, but the riffled current where the
river and Bogan meet over a large submerged rock make it
a concise target. Ham covered it first with a Black Dose,
then it was my turn with a Silver Gray and on my third
cast a strong fish took hold and fought hard to the head of
the pool; suddenly it bolted straight downstream seventy,
eighty yards until with a leap it disappeared into Deep
Pool, which with its many rocks extends a far way below
camp. I had watched him jump and knew it to be a bigger
salmon than we'd first seen. We should have bolted right
after him but Austie, alas, was taken short and had to go
ashore to relieve himself before we could proceed. "Keep
him taut, Mr. Weeks." Yes, but how at that distance with
a fish full of fight? I had a hundred feet of line out for
ten minutes and when at last we poled down to Deep
Pool the damage was done and the gut leader, a new Hardy
of 12 feet, parted. The salmon leapt once more to celebrate
his freedom and we could see how large he was. (We were
to see him upriver for the next two days, still on the surface
and impervious to flies as he worked mine out of his jaw.)
I reeled in what remained of my leader to find it had been
so chafed against the rocks that it could easily have broken
in two other frazzled places. Austie was full of apologies.

That night after supper all the captains attended a
council of war in the Admiral's cabin and at 11 P.M. it was
solemnly agreed that in view of Ted's loss we should renew
our assault for another forty-eight hours. The weather
favored us, first with rain, then by turning much colder.
Our supplies were nearly exhausted and again Austie's wife
helped out, this time with "a baked hen," a bird that had

done a lot of running before it reached the oven. But the strategy paid, for on our second morning Hoddy, the most deserving of us all, was in the driver's seat when John spotted a salmon in silhouette in Hale's Pool. It called for a cast of twenty-five feet, which can be deadly, and Hoddy's strong wrist made it so; from the observer's seat I was as excited as either of the actors and joined in their shout, when thirty minutes later the 14-pounder came into John's net. After all those fruitless days that was the memory we needed to bring us back.

Early in our stay Hoddy and I went downstream to try a pool of Jim Hayden's close to the settlement which we had leased for the day; it was very warm and some youngsters were in swimming at the mouth of Riley Brook. At sunset they went home and down to the stream came a twelve-year-old, barefoot, who baited his hook from his can of worms and proceeded to derrick in five as pretty trout as one could wish. It was the classic cartoon: the two sports with expensive gear and guide, flogging the water, catching nothing, while opposite, the barefoot boy took his limit. But if he, why not I? Next afternoon I put on my waders and said I was going to take time off from the canoe to explore Riley Brook. Don't wait supper.

It was not a very prepossessing stream as it was channeled by the sawmill to empty into the river, but the water felt mighty chill and that was a good omen. As the bathers were in the river again, this time with an inflated inner tube, I gave up any thought of casting the mouth and pushed inland across a meadow and then into the woods following a dim tote road and pausing now and then to eat the wild strawberries whose scarlet could be seen under the tall grass. No hurry; the sun was still high. The road divided and I continued up the right fork with the sound of the brook still in my ears until I had covered more than a mile; here I cut a diagonal down a soft swale and, taking care not to entangle my rod, ducked my way through the alders to the water's edge. At first sight the brook was wider, deeper and more clamorous than I had imagined. It had a rocky bottom and up ahead where it turned I could see a small crescent of sand.

Leaving a piece of bumwad on a forked stick to remind me of the exit, I entered the brook world, which is a sensuous one — even through the rubber waders the water says cold! In each run one feels the cool of the shade, the fragrance of the sun-warmed conifers — the breath of the brook — and sees the color of the water, golden in the rare clearings, blue-black where it cuts under the roots of a spruce. In nature's engineering it is always the biggest trees that fall, and their bulk athwart the stream forms bridges, forms islands, forms pockets where one supposes the larger trout lurk. These windfalls are sometimes powerful enough to divide the brook. I poked around at the head of an island where this had happened: a large hardwood provided the block for a dam of accumulated timber, mortised together by the spring run. With a stick I probed under the headwater and could not touch bottom; I thought of my young hero of yesterday and of what he could do with a worm on a hook and lead shot to sink it; drifting a Mickey Finn over these dark dungeons, as I tried to do, had no effect.

Except for the voice of the water the brook world is a solitary one in which a man's dimensions are ever changing. One moment you are striding along like Paul Bunyan in a dwarfed river; but as you climb over the hurdle of a fallen tree, being careful to place your weight on what looks sound, the rotted wood gives way and you plunge forward into an unsuspected pothole with a force that might have broken your leg. All conceit is jarred out of you; it is eerie and you are humble in such a wild place. What you look for is a pool with enough air room to cast, and in under the log not one but a clan of hungry trout. The one I located upstream was so rewarding that I knew I should have to return.

I went back two days later as the afternoon shadows were falling. I knew where the pools were now, and I was intent on exploring with my fly rod every nook and cranny of the upper reaches, lovingly and minutely. For the more open water I had a little red fly with a yellow body, and for the deep pockets along the bank and under tree roots a small brown hackle. Fishing is an act of privacy, and in a seclusion like this one naturally talks to oneself. Rather irritably for the most part, for the woods are always conspiring against you. The kingfisher has flown ahead giving his warning, but your real antagonists are the trees. You look behind you measuring the space for your backcast, and then facing front you concentrate on the square yard

of water where you mean to place your dry fly, not in midstream but as close to the bank as you dare. You strip off line and cock your wrist for the first cast — and at that point one of two enemies may intervene: the spruce at your back reaches out its arms to enmesh your leader, or the bank at which you are aiming pushes out a few inches further than you thought and snags your fly tight. The printable portions of your monologue sound like this: "There, right there, under the root . . . let it drift down to him . . . now . . . now . . . damn it, you're in the trees again . . . you can't lose that fly . . . will it pull out? . . . easy, now, easy . . . thank the Lord . . . now, not so much line, you fool . . . that's no good . . . get it closer to his hole . . . closer, closer . . . oh, you ass, you've caught the bank . . . boy, you certainly have the touch today . . ."

But once in a while you do have it; the little fly floats gently and the current edges it up to the door of the cavern; there is a flash of water, the glimpse of a pink belly, and you are fast to a brookie, the most beautiful and certainly the sweetest-tasting of any small fish.

Led by Matt's wife Gilly, the wives came up to inspect the camps, and the do-it-yourself regime was abandoned: help for the cooking and cleaning was found in the settlement, supper became the only movable feast, served before the evening fishing in the early summer and afterwards as the dark came earlier in September; and as a precaution against no-fish, a reserve of canned food and hard liquor was laid in. Children of fishing age joined the party and with so much space available the incoming and outgoing anglers overlapped for a reunion; birthdays were celebrated with broiled grilse, champagne, and cake with

candles, and the camp log which I had had bound and
presented to the Club in time for our first visit began to
fill out in several lively styles.

Of the many vignettes in mind I pick a few. There was
Matt White's feud with the hairy woodpeckers who insisted on drilling holes in his favorite stand of white birch;
after he had knocked off three with his .22 it settled down
to a regular Kentucky ambush. There was Matt's training
of his not-so-bright pointer, Jake, who was gunshy. There
would be the discharge; Jake would take off for the next
county and Matt would be left blowing his shrill whistle for
what seemed like hours. Of all the birdwatchers "Trudy"
Hammond was our best and it was a delight to walk with
her in June as she identified by the song; of the trout
fanciers none were as deft as "Bunny" Sargent, who had
learned the art of worming as a girl in Maine, and to rally
our spirits with Hearts, backgammon or fight-talk after a
day of defeat there was no one like "Bo" Amory. And always there was the recurrent question of whether we were
or were not poaching on Club waters. Two pools in particular were in dispute, Hale and Vanderbeck; the Club rarely
fished either with so much better available but wished to
make sure they could if the whim arose, while John, a loyal-

ist to the core, pressed for our advantage. I remember a formal call which the president of the Club made on Matt and how he came up to our landing just as I, on the opposite bank, was in the act of landing a good salmon. That it had been hooked in Deep Pool, right in front of camp, added to the persuasiveness of Matt's argument that we were law-abiding.

But the plain fact, reaffirmed with such wonderful patience in the log, was inescapable: the fishing was steadily declining. In our first year, when the bush pilots had been spraying the forest bordering the Tobique with DDT to wipe out the budworm, we were undeterred by the myriads of suckers who lay gasping and dying on the shoreline (at evening to be eaten like corn on the cob by the raccoons), and for a time we believed John when he said that the trout and salmon were unaffected. But when the pilots inadvertently sprayed the hatchery, and the congested pools of trout and parr turned belly-up we knew this was a deadly blight, if temporary. But the destructive impact of the dams on the salmon coming in from the sea was permanent and when a second, larger and deeper dam was foisted on the St. John at Beachwood, forty miles below Perth, old-timers on the Tobique gave the river up for lost. I heard them talking to John and there was no disguising their fatalism.

Beachwood Dam would be 100 feet high and instead of a fish ladder there would be an elevator which would open for fish in the center of the current and transport them to the top where they could be counted and released. (When the elevator failed to entice, some hundreds of fish were netted and shipped by tank trucks upstream. But this was ineffective.) Meanwhile the word went out among the natives: get down there and take what you can of the salmon that were milling and dashing themselves against the concrete. It won't be long.

I should have realized that what I was witnessing was the refinement of a process I had first seen on the West Coast: in this case, the extermination of Atlantic salmon by high-powered engineering. And when the monstrous new dam, Matquatoc, was authorized and the mechanical forces moved in to erect it on the St. John, eighteen miles from Fredericton, the extermination was final; the St. John, the Tobique and all the lesser tributaries have been wiped out as breeding rivers for the salmon in seventeen years. The fiction passes that such salmon as continue to approach Matquatoc will be netted and either stripped of their eggs or shipped by tank trucks far upstream. This is plain silly. Salmon aren't fools. They will have to go elsewhere and the survivors will.

"Who the hell's going to buy all this power?" asks Ham Robb. "Montreal, Maine, Quebec?" If they can distribute even a fair share of it, the proceeds and the make-work will have lessened the traditional poverty of the Maritimes, but it seems to me a pity that this benefit, if such it prove, should have been bought at such a price.

15. *THE DOCTOR AND THE RIVER*

IT seemed almost fated that Alex Bell should suffer
his first serious heart attack in the year when it was
discovered that the Northwest Miramichi was dying of
poison. It was a shock to realize that either of them, the
man or that glorious wild stream, was so vulnerable. All
his life Alex had looked and acted as if he were indestruc-

tible. Like many a great doctor before him he considered his own health last. Over the years, from Lillian Copp, Alex's secretary; from Howard and the other guides; from Jack Russell and from other natives of the north country, I had an accounting of what he meant to the Province. Dr. J. A. M. Bell, to give the full signature on his shingle, emerged from the Canadian Army at the end of the First World War a young stocky medico, eager for country practice, already well on the way to his shining baldness, with ruddy cheeks, and that welcoming smile that age was never to touch. His nature was sunny, but as I have said earlier, there was no more rugged fighter in the Maritimes. What he fought for was better health and education in an impoverished province, better hospitals — the Fredericton Polio Clinic is a monument to him — and clean-run, better-policed rivers.

Legends grew out of his hardihood and compassion, his willingness to answer any call. In the early days, when the snows were deep he went by sleigh, and returning, the seat and the runners would be crowded with schoolchildren he had picked up on the way home. Later, in a skimobile with skis in place of front wheels, he traversed the back roads which were otherwise impassable. He drove his cars the way he drove himself, unsparingly. He had the habit of rallying his patients and of checking up on them long afterwards; recovery was his mission, and not even his secretary could sum up the countless bills he did not collect. He would never accept a fee from students at the university. Many patients paid what they could in potatoes, as Cannie, his wife, who had to dispose of them, was well aware.

Alex's word was as good as his bond, and in time it covered the behavior of many. Among his patients in a small village at the mouth of the Miramichi was a huge family of French Canadians whom I shall call the Latourettes. During Prohibition, Papa Latourette made a pretty penny running rum from the French islands of St. Pierre and Miquelon. When Papa was captured and locked up in the jail in Newcastle, he sent for Alex. "Doctor, Doctor. I am not seek!" he kept repeating through the bars. "I not send for you because I am seek, Doctor, but because I cannot stay here in ze jail. My wife and family, she starve," and on Alex's word he went free.

The salmon river Alex loved best was the Northwest Miramichi, and to protect it Alex used persuasion, blasphemy, guile, personal intervention at Ottawa, and, when necessary, the arm of the law. I have stressed what eternal vigilance is needed to keep a salmon river alive. A balance must be struck between the trawlers patrolling the waters at the mouth and the owners of the set nets, some thirty miles of them, blocking two-thirds of the channel, through whose gauntlet the entering salmon must pass when the spring run is on. Alex fought for a Saturday-to-Monday lifting of all nets to make sure that enough mature fish would reach the spawning beds some eighty miles upstream. He fought against the irresponsible dumping of lignin from the pulp mills; he fought the lumber bosses for felling the shade trees on the banks of the redds in whose shadows the salmon spawned. He said of one supervisor, "The boy knew better than that. He is a trained biologist, a graduate of the university. He could perfectly well have left that fringe which shaded the spawning beds. But they put the heat on him at the home office and he looked the other way." Alex fought the poachers, who became desperate at times of unemployment. They work in teams of three or four at night, and a warden, who must go unarmed in New Brunswick, may lose an ear or an eye if he tries to interfere.

I was on the river that first summer when the budworm began ravaging the spruce in the 1950's. This was a recurring scourge and the last time it had hit, during the years of the First World War, the lumbermen had no defense except to cut as fast as they could and let the budworm destroy where it would. It took decades for the forests and the people who depend on them to recover from that scourge, and here it was again. But now we had the pesticides and especially the DDT spray, and Alex came up from Fredericton with a forestry consultant, Barney Flieger, to watch what was being done. Airstrips had been built for a squadron of dusters, and the planes, flying in tandem in the stillness of the evening, were drenching the forest with DDT. They flew just above the treetops, landing often with spruce branches in their landing gear; the pilots, many of them, were happy-go-lucky veterans of the Second World War, and they still rolled the dice with danger. The film of what they were dropping you could see on the surface of the water. "Will it save the trees?" I asked Barney. "We don't know," he replied, "but we think so." "What will it do to the fishing, especially the fingerlings, the parr?" "We don't know."

While I was in camp Barney went for long prowls through the timber, looking for old trees that might show

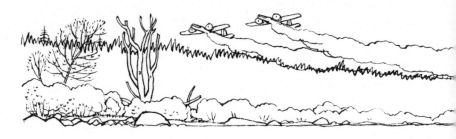

when the scourge had been here before. "Off in one knoll," he said that evening, "I found an old giant that suffered from this same blight at the time of Napoleon."

Alex watched all this in silence and with apprehension. He believed that the forest or that greater part of it which could be reached by the planes might be saved, as indeed it was. But he feared the aftereffects on the river. He noticed that the trout and parr lay dead on the banks, and he could not shake off the fact that the number of mature salmon began to diminish sharply the year after the spraying began.

Driving back from camp with him was an education. At sixty miles per hour and more his talk would range on the history of the valley; on the preservation of the elms, which in Fredericton are so beautiful; and on the guides and cooks, every one of them his friend, Howard and Henry and George and Art and Kathleen. They and their children mattered deeply to him, and he knew they kept him young.

Alex used to tease us about our Yankee veneration for royalty, but I remember how honored he felt when Princess Margaret took far more than the expected time to open the Polio Clinic in Fredericton, the clinic he had planned, equipped, and helped to finance.

The budworm was followed by an outburst of mining, and as the new mines were opened and old ones reactivated with such fresh hope in New Brunswick, Alex was quick

to appreciate the promise of prosperity, but it troubled him that the assayers and the mining engineers should be given such a free hand, free of Provincial regulation. A party of prospectors attended by French Canadians camped beside Black Pool, one of the Club's favorites, a pool almost completely shielded from the setting sun by a century-old pine. The Canucks felled the giant to make a footbridge, sawed off what wasn't needed and pushed the chunks into the pool. Alex was furious; he came down on them with a legal action and the fine, but the Black Pool was dead.

The zinc and copper mine which most affected the Northwest was not on the river itself but seven miles distant on a feeder brook which emptied into the river in mid-course. No provisions had been made initially to screen the waste water from the mine's operation, and when that which had been long standing in the corridors was pumped into the brook, it was lethal. The damage was not discovered until the early spring when the first run of salmon, some thirty mature fish, were counted through the fish box at the entrance to the Northwest, but instead of vanishing upstream, returned in thirty-six hours nosing for a way out. The biologists from St. Andrews who tended the fish box grew alarmed. Taking two pens of live fish, they placed one pen directly below where the brook flowed in, and the fish in that box were soon dead. The fish in the pen which was submerged upstream from the brook were full of life and were released. This pollution was the negation of every precaution for which Alex had fought: that Canada should so quickly surrender its civility and long-held conservation was a body blow.

After his first serious heart attack he would travel the distance from his office to Dam Camp in a Land Rover, equipped with shovel, axe, and sleeping bag in case of land-falls; he had been told not to fish but he came to see Howard and George and to hear the voice of the river. He had been told not to smoke cigars but he did not stop. Doctors knowing more about the inevitability find it harder to resign themselves than we innocents. One evening after a heavy thunderstorm he insisted on driving back to Fredericton in the Land Rover, but after a mile or so found his way blocked by a tree that had fallen. Out came the axe and he got to work on it. It was too much for him and when he made it back to camp there were fresh pains in his chest. He had to go at his own pace, close to the river he could not bear to leave.

16. *REVERIE*

THE rivers I have fished for three decades begin with
the North River where I had my baptism; the Ipswich
where I dove for my rod; the Rowley, the Ipswich, and the
Essex where I learned to watch for the seal, the tern, and
the striper; Kennebago stream where I first felt the power
of a landlocked salmon; and the Northwest Miramichi

where I was amazed by the wild intelligence of the Atlantic salmon. Since then I have fished the Diamond and the Blackwater in northern New Hampshire, the Battenkill and the Metawee in Vermont, Spruce Creek and the Loyalhanna in Pennsylvania, the Tobique, the broad Southwest, the Restigouche in New Brunswick, the Moisie in Quebec; in England the Tamar, the Dovey, the Test, and the Avon; the Boyne in Ireland, the Slava in Slovenia and the Cafe-au-lait in Tashkent, the Klamath, the Mackenzie, the Umpqua in Oregon; the White River in Colorado, the Campbell and the Gold in British Columbia. This is not a big inventory as anglers go, but for me it is the poetry of maturity.

I doubt if I shall ever outgrow the excitement bordering on panic which I feel the instant I know I have a strong, unmanageable fish, be it brook trout, brown trout, cutthroat, steelhead, or salmon, on my line. I know that I have acquired patience and the love of casting lightly and accurately whether or not the fish respond. I know that the hot blood has cooled and that I no longer reckon in terms of how many and how big. The river we love, the fish we admire, have given us an inestimable treasure, for when sight fails and one can no longer thread a fly even when peering at it against the evening sky, when the hearing dulls, when the legs are too weak for wading, we still have

the freedom to relive, not once, but again and again, the play of shadow and sunlight, the remembrance of fast water, and of that primitive strength which will move one's line almost beyond control.

In reverie, I like to remember how I began. Most of us make our approach to salmon fishing with very little or very old inherited equipment. On my second trip to the Northwest to fish with Jim White and his son Penny my armory consisted of the inexpensive Montague grilse rod, four flies, and two Hardy leaders. It soon became apparent that my poverty in leaders was inexhaustible. By the middle of the second day I had hung more of the gut in the trees than in the water. Jim patiently kept tying on new tippets for me, but they were fragile for anyone casting as I did, and in no time I would be reduced to the unbreakable minimum of four feet.

On the third day we arranged to boil the kettle at noon in company with the three Canadians who were fishing at the upper camp and it was my good fortune to sit beside Mr. De Forest, of blessed memory. Mr. De Forest was one of those anglers who had the best of everything and told you so: he began with his rod, moved on to his extra reels, and before we reached the doughnuts and tea, he pulled from his pocket the fattest pack of leaders I had ever seen — Fletcher & Fletcher Bivisible, these for heavy water, these for low, 9 feet and 12 feet, each in its folded envelope and beautiful! I couldn't have been more appreciative. When he pressed me to accept two of them for trial I did so with modesty, and glancing over at Jim White saw that he was determinedly looking upstream, with his jaw set in a hard line, and that Penny his son had flushed scarlet. With these rewards for my diplomacy the afternoon passed pleasantly.

At cocktails before supper Penny asked: "Pa, did you see what Uncle Ted did to poor old Mr. De Forest?"

"Yes," said Jim, "and I'd rather not talk about it."

I rejoice in the encounter with the forest lovers which occurred to my two sponsors in baptism, Ferris Greenslet, the editor, and Let Thompson, the artist. They were fond of fishing the West Branch of the upper Connecticut, and having a span of days they would lodge in a farmhouse, particular for its good meals, and in the morning they would drive to the bridge spanning their favorite stretch, park the car, and the one fish upstream, the other down until it was time for a late lunch and the nap. On the day I am describing their parking spot was preempted by a motorcycle with sidecar, and hanging from the handlebars was a woman's wicker basket containing a picnic lunch and a vanity case. The presence of young visitors did not deter the old boys and it being his turn Ferris started upstream. Ferris was a thorough, graceful fisherman, but he had risen nothing worth keeping until, as he approached the old apple trees of an abandoned farm, he spied the couple on the bank. (They did not see him, for whatever interest they may have had in trout had now been diverted to each other.) Ferris, realizing that he had verged on that adoration which is happiest when unobserved, about-faced and silently retreated. He cast his way back to the bridge with more than usual care and his artfulness was rewarded with a fine rainbow, going better than 21 inches, which went into his creel.

When Let rejoined him at the bridge, Ferris was congratulated on his fine fish and on the diplomacy of his disengagement upstream. Then together they reexamined the motorcycle. This time the picnic lunch and vanity case had vanished from the wicker basket and in their place was one 8-inch trout. Ferris removed the little fish and placed in its stead the big, lustrous rainbow, a proper gift.

Or I like to think of those two who taught me so much about the Canadian woods: Alex Bell and Howard Copp. I remember Alex's telling me of when, run down and sleepless from overwork, he had taken refuge for thirty days alone in the camp at Stony Brook, sleeping, cooking, fishing, living to himself and communicating with the river and the forest. How many men caught up in the tension of our times and distraught would find healing in such isolation? And I think of Howard, a guide at sixteen, veteran of many a log drive, father of eight children, an elder in the community, he whose philosophy has been shaped by the river and to whom it is insupportable that the salmon should ever cease running.

Howard is not easily taken by surprise, but twice I have shocked him. I am as I say an early riser and when I can't sleep I often take the river path to soak in the olive dawn and perhaps spot a fish. So I came silently along, studying Camp Pool and paused beside the guides' house just as Howard flung the contents of his shaving basin toward the stream. I caught it full and square in the face and after a startled moment his apology and my surprise blended in laughter.

The other occasion was at the end of an exhausting hot day after Howard, Fritzy and I had made a long expedition down to Stony Brook hoping to find a stray salmon in pools long untouched, and had found nothing. Henry was coming for us in the jeep and while we waited I peeled off my sweaty rubber waders and proposed to cool my legs in Wetmore's Pool. But the shale was cruel on my feet and I needed a stout branch with a fork to brace my rear and a taller crutch to take the weight of my left shoulder.

With these props I began casting with my right hand while Howard sat down speechless with amusement, said he'd never before seen a sport fish in his bare feet — and when I hooked a grilse and had to drop my supports and attend to the painful business in hand, he was chuckling, utterly delighted.

The rivers we love and the fish we admire — yes, but how long shall we have them? The Northwest Miramichi, which I love more than any other, has not recovered, nor will it: the lethal inflow from the mine has settled permanently into the banks of the feeder brook and at the brook's entrance to the river, and after each recurring high water the virulence, the percentage of lethal poisoning, rises to the point where such fish as have braved the river are driven back to the sea or destroyed. That wild and beautiful stream remains as a deadly sewer.

If my education as an angler has taught me anything it is this: that fresh waters anywhere in the United States and the wildlife within are in peril. Never in recorded history have men been so wasteful of their resources as have we in the United States. Not Egypt in its most magnificent dynasties nor Rome at the height of the Empire have been so wanton, so heedless of the future, so greedy for the quick profit as have we. The pollution of our most magnificent rivers by industrial and human waste; the saturation of our great lakes, ponds, and brooks by the inflow of pesticides with which we have been drenching our land; the lethal flow of poisoned water that flows not only from our mines but from those in Canada into any stream available form a chapter so devastating in its implications for the future that few, whether or not they be anglers, can read it without shuddering. We Americans are an impulsive people given to acts of unbelievable generosity, as witness the Marshall

Plan, yet we are capable in the same breath of denying to our conscience what we are doing to our own land.

It does not console me to think that my generation may be among the last to enjoy the vitality and beauty of our rivers; the dread of the desolation to come overshadows my personal delight. I do find hope in the statement of James Bryant Conant that the conversion of salt water into fresh will be an accomplished fact before the turn of the century. When this comes, when the miracle occurs, it will relieve the enormous pressure which we have put upon our streams. But will relief come too late? Or will the American conscience, impelled by a sense of outrage, rear up and form its legions, and with increasing political power, compel the regulation and the restoration so long overdue?

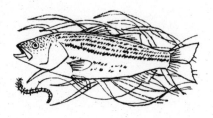